THE WONDERFUL DIFFICULT YEARS

RICHARD W. De HAAN

and

HERBERT VANDER LUGT

Published by
VICTOR BOOKS
a division of SP Publications, Inc.
Wheaton, Illinois

RICHARD W. DE HAAN is president and teacher of Radio Bible Class, Grand Rapids, Michigan. He is heard on hundreds of radio stations every week as well as on RBC's Sunday telecast, *Day of Discovery,* on a growing number of stations across the U.S. and Canada. *The Wonderful Difficult Years* is his most recent book. Others include *Israel and the Nations in Prophecy, The World on Trial, Happiness Is Not an Accident,* and *Satan, Satanism and Witchcraft.* Bible study books in a 32-page series include:

How to Have a Happy Home
The World's Last Hope
How to Make Sure of Heaven
How to Live with Yourself & Others
How to Study the Bible

CONTENTS

Grateful acknowledgment is hereby given for permission to reprint excerpts from the following:

Counseling Christian Parents, by William S. Deal, © 1970 by Zondervan Publishing House.

Jesus, the Man of Prayer, by John Henry Strong, published by The Judson Press.

Abortion: The Agonizing Decision, by David R. Mace, published by Abingdon Press.

"The Sexplosion," by Robert E. Fitch, from the Jan. 29, 1964, issue of *The Christian Century;* © 1964 by Christian Century Foundation.

Reality Therapy, by William Glasser, published 1965 by Harper & Row.

The Gospel of Matthew, by William Barclay, The Westminster Press, 1958.

THE WONDERFUL DIFFICULT YEARS

Published by Pyramid Publications for Victor Books, a Division of SP Publications, Inc.

First printing, June 1973

Library of Congress Catalog Card Number: 73-76814

ISBN 0-88207-241-2

Unless otherwise indicated, the Scripture quotations in this book are from **The New Scofield Reference Bible,** © 1967 by the Delegates of the Oxford University Press, Inc., New York. Quotations from the **New American Bible (NASB)** are by permission of The Lockman Foundation, La Habra, California.

Printed in the United States of America

BETTER PARENTS
RAISE BETTER CHILDREN

Today's philosophy of "doing your own thing" and its effects are still very much with us, tyrannizing our young with drugs, drink, fear and uncertainty; driving parents as well as their offspring to desperation and even despair.

This remarkable book offers help out of this destructive trend, through ageless biblical teachings which have given strength and character to countless generations.

Squarely confronting youthful rebellion, alienation from God and from society, sexual confusion and tragic mistakes, peer group pressures to conform, *The Wonderful Difficult Years* opens the door to the rich family relationship essential to successful parenthood and teen-age stability.

PREFACE

EVERYWHERE I go, I meet parents and church leaders who are eager for information which will enable them to meet the needs of our teens. Many excellent books and articles are available, some of them the products of Christian psychologists who write from the background of an excellent formal education and many experiences in the counseling room. These works contain a wealth of information and should not be ignored.

I am writing this book from the standpoint of a Bible teacher and father of four boys. I have tried to put into practice in my own home the fundamentals of child-rearing that are set forth in the Scriptures, and have developed a sympathetic understanding of the problems teen-agers face. I have also been appalled at some of the advice parents and young people receive from psychologists who have a completely naturalistic view of life, and I am afraid that some principles and methods which are definitely unbiblical have been adopted unwittingly by Christian people. I don't profess to have all the answers and certainly will not be able to tell adults what to do in every given situation, but I can set forth basic biblical concepts which can give clear guidelines to all who work with today's teens.

It is my prayer that this book will help parents better understand their teen-age sons and daughters as they pass through these wonderful, difficult years.

I am indebted to Herbert Vander Lugt, research editor of the Radio Bible Class, for the contributions he has made as we shared the responsibility of writing this book. I am also grateful to Clair Hess, who is RBC director of publications, and to consultant David Egner for their editorial work, and to Lois Weber for typing the manuscript.

RICHARD W. DE HAAN

1

CHOOSING FOR ETERNITY

PROBLEMS, problems, problems! That's what life sometimes seems to be for a young person actively involved in today's world. Yet we adults know from experience and observation that being a teen-ager can be an exciting and wonderful experience. Teen-agers are old enough to enjoy a measure of freedom from the continual supervision of parents and teachers, but young enough to be exempt from the heavy responsibilities of adulthood.

Generally, teens are happy with the daily routine of school and home life. Oh, they may complain about studies and homework, or talk about how boring certain classes are, but many like to learn new facts, and some really are happy about deepening their appreciation for the great works of art and literature.

Then, too, school life for our teens has many bright spots. There are rousing athletic events, exciting tournaments, class parties, rap sessions, and, of course, dates. Parents may have their misgivings about some of these activities, but for the well-adjusted young person they are great fun.

Not everything is bright and joyous for teen-agers,

however. Many adults look at them and say, "Those young people don't know how lucky they are. They have none of the cares and worries with which we are saddled." Such a remark reveals a woeful ignorance of what teens are going through.

Many teen-agers find life a bit scary, for they know they are no longer children and are painfully aware that they will be adults very quickly. They face a multitude of important decisions and don't feel ready to meet them. They often cover up their fears by putting on a bold and optimistic front because that's what everyone expects them to do, but deep inside they are in a state of turmoil.

Important questions keep begging for answers. What will the world be like 10 years from now? As they reflect upon these uncertainties, feelings of insecurity creep over them. Some of them "cop out" by losing themselves in the whirlwind activities of their peer group. And some teens who experiment with drugs, alcohol, and immoral living do so in an effort to escape their fears. But even when they do their best to banish disturbing thoughts from their minds, they experience a nagging uneasiness which comes from knowing they can't avoid adult responsibilities forever. Yes, it's wonderful to be a teenager, but it's difficult too.

As adult believers, we must give our young people guidelines by which they can gain a sense of direction and achieve spiritual, moral, and psychological stability.

WHAT ABOUT GOD?

The most important task of the Christian parent is to help his teen establish a real and satisfying individual relationship with God. As the young person reaches his teens, he must make a new commitment to God or renew the one he made as a child. This isn't always easy. Some young people are conformists by nature, and will say all the right things as taught at home and at church without possessing an experimental knowledge of them. They talk glibly, but they possess no reality. Christian parents must be able to detect such a spiritual and psychological state, and be certain that their children have every opportunity to enter into a deep, growing, independent relationship with God.

Recently a teen-ager newly enrolled in a Christian college came to her English professor deeply troubled. She had been raised in a Christian home and had attended a Bible-believing church regularly. But now, away from her home and her high school friends, she was faced with the responsibility of making her own decisions and determining her own relationship with the Lord. God just didn't seem real to her, and she pleaded, "Please show me God! I've got to know that He exists. I'm not sure of anything anymore! Oh, I know all about God, but I don't know Him at all. Please, please show me God!"

This young lady had found it easy to let her parents and her church assume that she had been growing in the Lord. They took it for granted that because she attended the youth group functions and was obedient at home she was maturing spiritually.

In actuality, she had merely been going through the motions. Now, having enrolled in a Christian college where she met many young people who had developed a deep and satisfying individual relationship with God, she recognized her own shallowness. She discovered that she didn't really know how to pray and determine God's will. She was literally crying out for help.

Many other young people who grow up in our churches are too concerned about a multitude of personal problems to give much thought to the nature of their faith. The difficulties they face day by day are so pressing that spiritual matters take a place of low priority in their thinking.

Teen-agers aren't expecting to die soon. The anticipation of many years of living concerns them far more than an improbable early death. They are more worried about being accepted by their peers or passing some of the courses with which they are having difficulty.

They are trying to get along with their parents, They are under pressure to use drugs and are won-They are under pressure to use drugs and are wondering how far they can go with the crowd that thinks it's cool to experiment with them. They have sexual drives that need to be understood and controlled. They have a desire to love and be loved.

These problems confront our youth every day, and they are very, very important to them. Thus it is easy for them to postpone making a serious decision about God and His will until these other difficulties are resolved.

THE IMPLICATIONS OF NATURALISM

The truth is, however, that young people can never understand themselves nor solve their problems until they determine what they will do about God. A decision to believe on Him as He is revealed in the Bible will influence every choice they make. As parents or leaders, we must show them why they ought to commit themselves to the way of faith in God.

We need to let our young people know that Christianity, as a revealed religion, is centered in Jesus Christ, the Son of God. We must make it very plain that faith is not just an isolated fragment in the total construct of their lives, but that belief in Jesus involves a total relationship, reaching and stabilizing every facet of their existence. We must urge them to give themselves over to the Lord, and we must show them that the life of faith provides direction for the academic and social as well as the spiritual areas of their life.

We should also consider with them the alternative to living a life based upon belief in the Almighty, making it plain to them that the denial of God carries with it a number of critical implications. If one does not believe in God, he must view human beings as the products of blind evolution—mere accidents of nature without meaning or purpose.

Every young person should be made to see that, logically, a completely naturalistic view can lead only to despair. If one doesn't believe in God, he ought to feel sorry for himself and envy the animals. After all, they don't have the worries and cares of humans, and according to the naturalists they are just as well off in the end.

Man's special problem is that he thinks about himself and his destiny. Some secular writers refer to him as "garbage," and declare frankly that the more one understands his real situation as a "thinking animal," the more miserable he becomes. The ultimate conclusions of naturalism are frightening!

EVIDENCES OF DESPAIR

The concept of man as an absurd creature has made its mark in our society. We see one manifestation of it in people whose personal appearance has been allowed to degenerate. Dirty clothes, unwashed bodies, uncombed hair often constitute outward evidence of an inner feeling of despair and worthlessness. Why should one dress up or keep clean when he feels he is nothing but garbage?

Parents and church leaders must point this out to our youth and help them understand why some people behave and talk the way they do. We can implant in their consciousness reasons for cleanliness, good grooming, and consideration of others.

You see, Christians do not consider people, even the most depraved, to be trash; nor do they deem themselves to be worthless or their lives to be without meaning.

The drug culture is another outgrowth of the idea that human beings are merely thinking animals with no significance and no eternal future. Thousands of young people who feel unwanted and alone are experimenting with dangerous drugs, though they know this practice will cut down their life expectancy. Perhaps unwittingly, they are saying it is better to escape reality through drug-induced trips and die young than to face the truth as it is and live to a ripe old age. Now, this attitude might make sense if we were only an accidental product of the evolutionary process, but when one recognizes the existence of God and believes that human beings have been placed upon this earth for a purpose, he certainly cannot agree with such a despairing outlook.

As Christian parents or counselors, we must recognize that it is natural for many young people to feel helpless and inadequate. After all, they are faced with the demands of their peers and the prospect of entering into the adult world with its many responsibilities for which they do not think they have been equipped.

In their intense desire to be accepted, young people make mistakes and suffer the consequences of inexperience and poor judgment. If not treated correctly at this time, they can easily begin to think of themselves as misfits and failures. A young man recently said to a friend, "I can't do anything right. I try to please my parents, but just when things are going well I botch it all up. No matter what I do, it always seems to be wrong. I guess I'm just no good, and never will be."

This kind of thinking plays right into the hands of those who deny God's existence, say that life has no meaning, and encourage our youth to turn to drugs, sex, or crime. We must show our teens that they are of tremendous worth, not only to us but also to God, who sent His Son to die for them. When we must correct them, we should do so in love and not tear down their self-respect and sense of individual importance.

ONLY ONE GOOD CHOICE

We should lead our teen-agers to understand that man has only two alternatives, and that the choice of one or the other makes all the difference in the world. A person must either accept the existence of God as a fact or conclude that we are meaningless accidents, programmed machines, absurdities in a world doomed to oblivion, creatures for whom death is the only release from the tragedy of existence.

No other option is available. One must either adopt the philosophy of naturalistic evolution or believe in God. He must view human beings as nothing more than garbage or see them as intelligent and responsible moral creatures for whom God has a wonderful purpose.

The book of Proverbs contains many wise declarations, but none is more important than this: "The fear of the Lord is the beginning of wisdom, and the knowledge of the Holy One is understanding" (Prov. 9:10). The first step toward a life that is good, worthwhile, and filled with joy is to say, "I believe in God. I acknowledge that He loves me, and that I am worth enough that His Son died to redeem me. I will live to serve Him."

REASONS FOR BELIEF

When young people ask us to give them reasons for making a definite affirmation of faith in God, our response must place the greatest emphasis upon the revelation He has given in the Bible. We who know Christ believe the Scriptures to be true because the Holy Spirit spoke to us through them, and when we obeyed them by acknowledging our sinfulness and accepting Jesus as our Savior, we experienced deliverance from sin's guilt and power. Our faith in the Bible, however, is not a blind leap in the dark. The Bible is an authentic record of God's activities upon our planet, and its reliability and truthfulness are confirmed in many ways.

The events that took place from the time of Abraham onward fall within the scope of historical research, and the truth of many biblical incidents is confirmed by their presence in ancient records other than the Holy Scriptures. If one can look upon the accounts of the rise and fall of Assyria, Babylonia, Persia, Greece, and Rome as reliable, he should be able to do the same with the Old Testament. In fact, when one examines the Old Testament carefully and notes the prophecies that were fulfilled in an amazing manner, he cannot but conclude that this document is unusual, to say the very least.

For example, Ezekiel 26 records the prophetic declaration concerning Tyre. The prophet foretold Nebuchadnezzar's attack upon the city, and declared that he would destroy it. This prediction came to pass within a few years, but one aspect of Ezekiel's prophecy remained unfulfilled. He had said, ". . . and they shall lay thy stones and thy timber and thy dust in the midst of the water" (Ezek. 26:12). Nebuchadnezzar did not place the stones, timber, and dust into the water.

In fact, though he destroyed the city, Nebuchadnezzar did not capture many of its inhabitants, for they fled to a small offshore island. There they built a new city, and for a long time it appeared as though Ezekiel's prophecy that the old city would be scraped flat would not come to pass.

In 334 B.C., however, Alexander the Great ordered his soldiers to gather the ruins of the old coastland city and dump them into the water. His men even scraped the ground down to bare rock and used the materials to build a causeway to the island. The Greek armies then marched into the island city and captured it. To this day, the coastal city of Tyre has not been rebuilt. The bare rock where it once stood is silent but eloquent testimony to the truthfulness of God's Word.

The New Testament, which even its critics now acknowledge was written by contemporaries of Christ, is also a reliable and trustworthy document. When you read it without a spirit of antagonism toward its message, you cannot help but be impressed that its writers were not expressing mere ideas, but reporting actual events and recording messages Jesus really spoke. The early Christians, who were accused of "turning the world upside down" (Acts 17:6), were able to face bitter persecution and death itself with a radiant and joyous spirit because they had experienced newness of life through a personal encounter with the living Christ.

Our youth can be made to see that unbelievers, who blandly assert that God doesn't exist and that, if He does, we cannot know what He is like, are ignoring a body of evidence that deserves careful consideration.

We must avoid one common mistake in presenting our reasons for faith in God. Some people try to prove His existence as a scientifically demonstrable fact, but a bright young person has studied enough to know that this is a subject beyond the reach of the scientific method. After all, we cannot take historical events or abstract things such as faith and prayer into a laboratory and test them repeatedly as we do physical elements in order to prove God's existence.

While it is well for us as adults to acknowledge that we are unable to demonstrate God's reality in a scientific manner, we can insist that we have good evidence for belief. Our youth must be made to realize that everyone, both theist and atheist, lives by some form of belief. The atheist takes his position by faith, just as much as the one who says, "I believe in God." But the atheist cannot offer as many good reasons for his unbelief as the Christian can for his faith.

We have already stated that belief in a Designer and Creator of the universe enables one to develop a satisfying philosophy of life. In contrast, the acceptance of naturalism can only lead to a sense of utter futility and despair. This is reason enough to commit oneself to faith in God. Other valid grounds for this step can also be given. The believer can present a better explanation of how the universe came into being, and a more reasonable interpretation of man's distinct advantages over the animal, than can the unbeliever.

One may think it is inconsistent for us to affirm that we cannot scientifically prove God's existence to an unbeliever, and then proceed to point out reasons for belief. But this isn't the case. We are led to faith through the Holy Spirit's convicting and enlightening ministry through the Scriptures, but we make our decision in a rational manner. We can give good grounds for belief. Peter declared, "But sanctify the Lord God in your hearts, and be ready always to give an answer to every man that asketh you a reason of the hope that is in you, with meekness and fear" (1 Peter 3:15).

Yet Paul also made it clear that sheer faith without demonstrable proof is an indispensable factor in the believer's life. He said, "For we walk by faith, not by sight" (2 Cor. 5:7). He also emphasized that faith does not come primarily through the intellect.

Thus he refused to approach the people in Corinth with eloquence or a display of great learning, because he did not want their faith to be based upon these human factors but to be the result of the supernatural activity of God. "And my speech and my preaching were not with enticing words of man's wisdom, but in demonstration of the Spirit and of power; that your faith should not stand in the wisdom of men, but in the power of God" (1 Cor. 2:4, 5).

We as parents must also depend primarily upon the Holy Spirit, praying and using the Scriptures to bring spiritual help to our teens, and using arguments for the faith only as confirmatory evidences.

ORDER AND DESIGN

The created world itself strongly suggests that it has been planned by a Master Designer. Even the most simple elements are extremely complex. For example, the typical protein molecule, which is essential to life, is made up of 3,000 atoms, and the odds against one of them being formed accidentally are astronomical. In this case, the law of mathematical probability argues eloquently *for* the existence of God.

We find ourselves thinking instinctively of the Almighty when we observe the beauties of the earth and the grandeur of the heavens. Our inner being responds with great feeling when we read the words of the Psalmist, "The heavens declare the glory of God, and the firmament showeth His handiwork. Day unto day uttereth speech, and night unto night showeth knowledge" (Ps. 19:1, 2). Yes, the intricate beauty and complexity of our world give evidence of a Master Designer.

HUMAN INTELLIGENCE AND ASPIRATION

A second reason for believing in God's existence is the nature of man. No human being can help but reflect upon himself. He knows that he is a rational creature able to make intelligent decisions. He wonders about the meaning of life, questions the rightness and wrongness of his own conduct and that of others, possesses a fear of death, and has a curiosity to know what lies beyond the grave. If one does not accept the existence of a personal God, he can offer no explanation for man's intelligent and moral consciousness.

Therefore, when our young people have doubts about God, we should discuss with them the profound thoughts and deep feelings that are expressed in the works of art, music, poetry, and religion. A young person willing to exercise his mind is not apt to conclude that beings with such capacities are merely creatures of chance. Young people will recognize that the likelihood of their having been created and endowed by God is far greater than its alternative—blind chance. The ability of man to perceive beauty is evidence of a Being who gives the criteria for beauty: God himself.

This need for meaning and purpose expresses itself in a number of ways. It can be seen in the emotional unrest of our times. Many deep thinkers are in a state of total despair because they find it almost impossible to face existence in a world which they consider to be a mere accident. Even the young people with their idealistic espousal of love and peace are implicitly acknowledging their need for faith in the existence of One who can give to life its ultimate significance and meaning.

Every normal human being must at some time or other take a step of faith, either in the direction of God or of atheistic naturalism. Our youth must realize that it makes far better sense to believe in God than to deny His existence. Faith in Him provides a satisfying world-and-life view, a logical explanation of origins, and a more realistic interpretation of human nature. The person who declares, "I believe in God," and then carries out the moral and spiritual implications of this affirmation, has nothing to lose and everything to gain. The person who does not, possesses no satisfying answers to the problems of his existence and no hope for the future.

WHAT IS GOD LIKE?

Having concluded that God exists, the next question that inevitably arises is, "What is He like?" To answer this query, we can turn to four areas for information—nature, man's personality, history, and the Bible.

HE IS POWERFUL AND RATIONAL

First, we may look to the universe for clues, and in its vastness, intricacy, and orderly design we see indications that its Maker is powerful and rational. Many physicists who consider themselves skeptics speak of a materialistic "law" which governs everything. In so doing, they are really positing the existence of a supreme power of some kind. They may not attempt to define what they mean, but they acknowledge the necessity for an intelligence that is somehow involved in or with the world.

Paul said that the created universe speaks of God's might and wisdom. "For the invisible things of Him from the creation of the world are clearly seen, being understood by the things that are made, even His eternal power and Godhead, so that they are without excuse" (Rom. 1:20). Therefore, it is perfectly logical to say that the intricately constructed atom tells us that God is powerful and rational.

HE IS A MORAL BEING

We can find another clue to God's character by studying our own psychological makeup. As human beings, we have a conscience which tell us that some things are right and others are wrong. This conviction of moral values is etched so deeply into human nature that it cannot be removed. Even the most primitive people possess these qualities. This indicates that the God who made man is a moral Being, for a blind and impersonal Fate could not have injected this element into humanity.

Paul affirmed that a holy God is responsible for man's deep feelings about right and wrong. "For when the Gentiles, who have not the law, do by nature the things contained in the law, these, having not the law, are a law unto themselves; who show the work of the law written in their hearts, their conscience also bearing witness, and their thoughts the meanwhile accusing or else excusing one another" (Rom. 2:14, 15).

The fact that man's spiritual sensitivity indicates the existence of a moral Creator was declared by Dr. Ralph Wyckoff, professor in the Department of Physics at the University of Arizona, to a convention of scientists in 1967:

There have . . . always been men of high and disciplined spirituality who have insisted on their direct experience of something greater than themselves. Their conviction of the reality of a spiritual life apart from and transcending the life of the body may not lend itself to scientific proof or disproof; nevertheless the remarkable transformation in personality seen in those who rightfully lay claim to such experience is as objective as tomorrow's sunrise. Millions of lesser men draw strength from the contacts they can make through prayer and meditation with this aspect of the inner life. (Quoted by Mr. J. Philip McLaren in *Journal of the American Scientific Affiliation,* September 1968, p. 72)

Man's moral and spiritual qualities, therefore, teach us that the God who made him is a moral Being.

HE IS RIGHTEOUS AND JUST

A third source of knowledge about God is human history, which confirms the testimony of man's own nature, that God is a moral Being, and sets Him forth as the righteous and just Governor of the universe. The principle expressed in the Bible, "Be sure your sin will find you out" (Num. 32:23), has been proven again and again.

One of our contemporary scholars has said, "When you slide against the grain of the universe, you get splinters." Not all historians are willing to make this admission, but the fact remains that whenever a nation has become morally decadent, it has lost its power and grandeur. We believe this to be a partial revelation of God's holiness.

Young people especially are conscious of overwhelming feelings of guilt that engulf them at certain moments. The nagging, inescapable sense of wrongdoing, even though masked by an appearance of self-assurance, is clear evidence of the holiness of God as expressed through conscience and emotion. We should point this out to them as a further reason for faith in God, and as an indication that He is indeed a moral Being who is concerned about their conduct.

HE IS THE GOD OF THE BIBLE

Though nature, man's personality, and history tell us a great deal about God, a truly satisfying knowledge of Him is impossible without the Bible. It teaches us about creation, the entrance of sin into the world, and God's program of redemption.

We cannot fully comprehend everything the Bible says about the Lord, but we can know enough to meet the deepest needs of the heart. If we believe what the Word of God declares and live in obedience to it, we can enjoy fellowship with God, and possess inner peace and vibrant hope.

WHO IS JESUS CHRIST?

When anyone, young person or adult, begins to think about God and reads the Bible for information, he comes face to face with the question, "Who is Jesus Christ?"

No one who is really seeking the answer to spiritual and moral questions can avoid a serious consideration of Jesus of Nazareth. He is the central figure of the entire Bible. The Old Testament sets forth His person and work in types and figures, and contains literally hundreds of specific prophecies of His coming. The New Testament relates the story of His birth, life, death, resurrection, and ascension to Heaven, declares His teachings, and explains the significance of all He said and did.

These documents are now known to have been in existence and in circulation long before the first century ended, and therefore must be considered authentic and reliable. Besides, the coming of Jesus Christ brought about revolutionary changes in society. Therefore, we have ample material on which to base a conclusive answer to the question about the identity of Jesus Christ. We need to make our youth realize that their faith centers in this Person, the Son of God and Savior of sinners.

THE NEW TESTAMENT WITNESS

The Gospels tell us that, in fulfillment of Old Testament prophecy, Jesus was born of a virgin in Bethlehem, fled to Egypt to escape Herod's wrath, and grew up in Nazareth as an obscure worker in a carpenter shop.

At the age of 30, Jesus began His public ministry. He called together a small band of followers, taught spiritual truths that exuded the very breath of

Heaven, performed miracles, and lived a life marked by spotless purity and perfect love. He claimed to be God, declaring, "Verily, verily, I say unto you, Before Abraham was, I am" (John 8:58).

He also said that He had come to die for sinners and that He would rise again. No one fully understood Him. His enemies determined to get rid of Him, and the religious leaders of His day were finally able to bring about His crucifixion on a Roman cross. But three days later His tomb was empty, and His followers were declaring joyously that they had seen Him in His resurrection body and had talked to Him.

After 40 days of appearing to His disciples and instructing them, He ascended to Heaven in a physical manner. On the day of Pentecost, the Holy Spirit came upon the disciples and they began to preach the Gospel of a resurrected Christ with such power that they turned the world of that day upside down. Since that time, multitudes from every race and station in life have trusted Jesus Christ and found assurance of forgiveness, peace with God, and a power to live victoriously.

Our young people today will find it quite fashionable to speak of Jesus of Nazareth as a wonderful person, the greatest and purest man who ever lived. Even some of the extreme revolutionaries like to claim that they are following His example. The tragedy is that most of these people do not recognize Him for what He really is. They have never considered the total witness of the New Testament, and therefore do not see Him as a Person of the divine Trinity who became a member of the human family in order that He might be our Savior and King. They do not realize that, through Him, God came into our space-time world to show us what He is like and to provide salvation from sin.

Therefore, we must make our young people understand, both through our words and our example, that when one believes in Christ as He is revealed in the Bible, he can find peace with God and hope for eternity. Jesus Christ himself declared, "I am the way, the truth, and the life; no man cometh unto the Father, but by Me" (John 14:6).

In summary, you and I, who are responsible for helping our young people, must show them the need for making or renewing certain basic spiritual commitments. We must urge them to take a step of faith and believe in God. We must enable our young people to understand that the Christian faith is reasonable. They should know that some of the world's leading scholars unhesitatingly declare their belief in the message of the Bible. But they must also be challenged, "Taste and see that the Lord is good" (Ps. 34:8).

We must also show them in our own lives the wonderful results of a sincere faith in the living Christ. They can then discover for themselves that He gives deliverance from the sins that destroy, and freedom from the bondage of drug addiction, lust, fear, and uncertainty. When they make these discoveries, they can become examples to their peers. They will be able to show them that true happiness is found in obedience to the moral and spiritual principles set forth in the Bible.

2

MORAL PRINCIPLES—
Secular Versus Christian

NOTHING is more pathetic than a wasted life. This is true whether a person dies at a ripe old age or in his youth, but somehow it hits us harder when we see a *young person* who has destroyed himself.

As I write, I am thinking of a man in his early twenties, weakened in body and mind because of drug abuse, who asks desperately, "Where did I go wrong?" At an age when he should be enjoying life and eagerly anticipating the future, he finds himself empty and without hope.

His home has been broken by divorce, and he has been forgotten by most of his friends. He has lost one job after another, and now no one will hire him. His spirit is crushed, and his physical health is broken. When he dares to look ahead, he sees only the black agony of loneliness and despair.

In one respect, however, he is fortunate—he is still alive and can find deliverance if he will turn to Jesus Christ. Many of his peers who chose the same downward path have already died.

Let us think again about the pathetic query he raised, "Where did I go wrong?" Did his misfortune start when he told his first lie as a little boy? When

27

he smoked his first cigarette? Or did his downfall begin when he became intoxicated the first time?

It's hard to put a finger on the turning point in a person's life. Maybe events from his childhood have left scars that cannot be fully removed. Possibly his parents should bear some of the blame. It is not at all unlikely that wrong companions led him astray, and that an unfortunate marriage compounded his problems.

The reasons for his present state may be many and complex, but for such a person the question, "Where did I go wrong?" is not nearly so important as "Where do I go from here?"

The right kind of counseling could help him, but if he went to someone who diagnosed him as neurotic and proceeded to dig into the reasons for all of his problems, he might find excuses for his wrong conduct but never change. Chances are that he will not sincerely seek deliverance until deep feelings of guilt, a consciousness of vast emptiness in his life, and the fear of what lies ahead drive him to the point of total despair. Only then will he be open to receive the help he needs, acknowledging his sinfulness and making a genuine commitment to Jesus Christ.

Christians with sons or daughters who have gone down the road toward physical and spiritual destruction may feel completely helpless and wonder what to do. Actually, as we shall see in a later chapter, a great deal can be done. Prayer and an attitude of kindness and helpfulness will work wonders. It is too late for mere parental advice, but prayer, love, communication, and a good example may be used of the Lord to bring that young person to himself.

A wise parent will avoid badgering a teen-ager with recriminations, which will most likely drive him farther and farther from the help you are trying to give him. He is not thinking as you are. His view of life, though erroneous, is all-important to him, and unless he is in some kind of serious trouble he really doesn't want to change right now. He will effectively shut you off if you nag or scream at him, but he cannot close his heart to your love, your prayers, and your manifestations of continuing concern for him.

Remember, God's Word teaches that the sons and daughters of godly and praying parents will have difficulty continuing in a life of sin, and will find it hard to remain away from God. The influence of early years and the ministry of the Holy Spirit will permeate their inner thoughts, filling them with misery and unrest, and showing them their need of the Savior.

Our main concern in this chapter, however, is not to give information about reclaiming those who have fallen deeply; instead, we want to show how to prevent young people from reaching this place of desperation. If we give them a solid spiritual foundation in the home and church while they are small children, and show them love and understanding in their teens, the chances of their becoming the human wrecks we have described are greatly decreased.

That is why godly parents are so important. The father and mother who have chosen the Christian pathway can profoundly influence their offspring. True, some young people will still experiment and learn certain lessons the hard way, and a small percentage will go through periods of intense intellectual and emotional turmoil, but the general direction of life is usually determined before a young person has gone through his teens.

Let us now consider some of the basic biblical truths we can give our sons and daughters to insure that they will have real insight and understanding as they face the prevailing secular philosophies. They need to know these three facts about life: (1) that human wisdom has always failed, (2) that a life given over to pleasure ultimately brings frustration, and (3) that the best systems of ethics the world can devise are disappointing and ineffectual.

At first sight you may think that this is heavy material to discuss with your younger teens, but you will find your fears unfounded. We tend to underestimate the ability of our teen-agers to reason, and we often do not realize how deeply concerned they are about the basic issues of life and conduct.

THE INADEQUACY OF HUMAN WISDOM

A foundational truth we parents must impress upon our sons and daughters is that human wisdom has always failed to meet man's deepest needs. This knowledge will help them as they begin to grapple with the teachings of people who take a completely naturalistic view of life.

Young people have a tendency to be optimistic, idealistic, and impressionable. They are taught to have a great deal of confidence in what they hear and read outside the home and church. Since most of the textbooks they use are written from the standpoint of naturalism, and the majority of the teachers in our public schools are not Christians, our youth who sincerely want to know what is true will face some perplexing problems and difficult decisions.

HANDLING AN INTELLECTUAL PROBLEM

A 15-year-old boy, for example, may come home from school and say that he is convinced that man has been on earth for more than one million years. He may declare that this makes it difficult for him to believe what the Bible says about Adam and Eve. When he talks this way, you can make serious mistakes in your reaction to him, either by showing angry indignation and speaking emotionally or by posing as an expert when you really don't have all the facts.

First, do not become incensed with your son's

statement and make strong assertions about unbelieving teachers and scientists. Do not overstate the case when you talk about the mistakes men of science make. True, the non-Christians among them are spiritually blind, and some of their theories do appear ridiculous when placed alongside the biblical explanations. But teen-agers know that scientific discoveries have led to tremendous technological advances, and all your emotionally charged and dogmatic assertions will not convince them that you are right and their teachers are wrong.

If man's knowledge is doubling every 10 years, he must be finding many, many new facts and learning new information about every field. This, of course, will mean changes in textbooks and new data being presented in classrooms. Your child is probably more aware of these new discoveries than you are, and is informed about them by excited young teachers enthused about their subjects. They should not by any means be dismissed by a shrug of the shoulders. Besides, your young person will sense it if you are overstating your case.

Your son or daughter will not be helped if you pose as an expert when in reality you know very little about the subject or are misinformed. Your teen will respect you more if you admit that your knowledge in a particular scientific or technological field is limited than if you speak authoritatively, trying to tell him exactly what he must believe and making foolish blunders while doing so.

Actually, your teen-ager is looking for reassurance. He wishes to be given added reasons to believe that the faith he has been taught at home and in church is not in jeopardy. You can strengthen him by reminding him that numerous outstanding men in the areas of physics, biology, chemistry, and anthropology find no conflict between the Christian faith and their field of study.

When our sons and daughters realize that these

recognized experts are loyal to the Bible as the Word of God and to Jesus Christ as their Savior, they will not feel that their faith is threatened. Rather, they will be strengthened and challenged to continue in their beliefs about God and the world. Their confidence in us and in the church will be increased.

Remember, our teen-agers do not really want to believe that they are mere creatures of chance whose existence will end at death. Because they live in a world in which tremendous scientific accomplishments are being made, however, they can't help but be impressed by the claims of naturalistic scientists.

They have been informed that, before long, computer libraries and microfilm reference works will electronically dispense organized information on every subject into homes and schools. They have heard that some scientists say they will soon be able to reproduce people through the process of cloning. It is said that future control of genetics will be so complete that biologists will be able to bring into existence either a generation of people with very high I.Q.'s or a race of slaves.

We ought to do our best to encourage our teens to talk to us about these matters. We should readily acknowledge that such developments will present problems in the area of Christian ethics—problems which must be faced—but at the same time we should show them that we have absolute confidence that God is in complete control of His world, and that the Christian faith will never be destroyed, and that the wisdom of man will ultimately fail to produce the solution to his problems.

THE BIBLICAL TESTIMONY

The Apostle Paul declared that the Gospel of Christ, which the intellectuals of his day despised as being unworthy of consideration, accomplished what all of mankind's wisdom had failed to do. It brought deliverance from sin, freedom from fear, and a joyous outlook to thousands during the first century of the Christian era, and actually changed the course of history.

The Apostle said, "For the preaching of the cross is to them that perish foolishness; but unto us who are saved it is the power of God. For it is written, I will destroy the wisdom of the wise, and will bring to nothing the understanding of the prudent. Where is the wise? Where is the scribe? Where is the disputer of this age? Hath not God made foolish the wisdom of this world?

"For after that, in the wisdom of God, the world by wisdom knew not God, it pleased God by the foolishness of preaching to save them that believe. For the Jews require a sign, and the Greeks seek after wisdom; but we preach Christ crucified, unto the Jews a stumbling block, and unto the Gentiles foolishness; but unto them who are called, both Jews and Greeks, Christ the power of God, and the wisdom of God" (1 Cor. 1:18-24).

When Paul wrote these words, the civilized world was characterized by social unrest, moral disorder, and religious pessimism. All the sagacity and grandeur of Greek philosophy and literature, combined with the organizational genius of Rome, had failed to lead mankind into happiness.

The three great philosophies of the day—Stoicism, Epicureanism, and Hedonism—were very similar to the current popular views of life. Each of these maintained that man could not possibly know truth. Therefore, each offered to man what it hoped would be a way to cope with life's problems, whether by blind acceptance of fate or by escape through intellectual or physical pleasure. The result was that moral deterioration and a general spirit of gloom prevailed.

When the apostles preached the Gospel of a resurrected Christ, however, they brought joy, satisfaction, and hope into the lives of all who believed their message. Skepticism was replaced by assurance, and the true meaning of life obtained through faith in Christ brought about an end to unhappiness and sin for many people.

THE PRESENT HOPELESSNESS

A feeling of emptiness and frustration hangs heavy over the world today as well. The most prevalent philosophy is existentialism, which affirms that we must accept life as meaningless—even absurd. It also claims that somehow through a nonrational feeling or act we must make some kind of assertion or seek an experience by which we will be "authenticated as individuals."

This trend in thinking has resulted in the emergence of the "now" generation. The search for "authentication of existence" has caused young people to forsake the past and close their eyes to the future. Their eager quest is to find meaning for the present only—and this usually through pleasure. If "right now" somehow has significance for them, they are happy, and they will go to any extreme and try everything they can to obtain that fleeting moment of satisfaction.

But this so-called experience is really only a *feeling* without any logical basis. Existentialists believe, however, that it is better than its alternative; namely, sheer desperation. Most current philosophers do not believe there are any logical answers to the great questions: Who are we? Why are we here? Where are we going?

Our young people must be shown how totally unsatisfactory this empty view of life is. It must be demonstrated to them in very convincing terms that man cannot just turn his back upon the events of the past. Much can be learned regarding the meaning of life and solutions for problems when one reviews history and literature, willing to learn from man's mistakes and previous achievements. Furthermore, a great many people have sacrificed their lives to bring about the advances in science, technology, and medicine we now enjoy.

Our young people also should be reminded of the importance of the future. The happiness of their later years and the prospects of life after death are deeply influenced by what happens now, and are to be carefully prepared for.

"Now" is not the only moment of importance. If our ancestors had lived without regard for the future, where would we be today? Against this background our teens will be able to see how wonderful it is to know the answer to the enigmas of life through faith in Jesus Christ as He is revealed in the Scriptures.

SCIENTIFIC KNOWLEDGE IS INCOMPLETE

We can also point out to our young people that every discovery in the field of science leads to further complexities for which we have no satisfactory account. Men are still far from understanding the mystery of life, and they have no real explanation for the origin of existence. Much of the material about man's findings and expectations set forth in newspapers, magazines, and paperbacks is unreliable and should not be taken seriously. Moreover, scientific knowledge has been unable to solve man's basic needs as a person who wonders why he is here, where he is going, and how he should live.

SOCIAL SCIENCES HAVE FAILED

As philosophy and the material sciences have not produced happiness, so the social sciences have also proven deficient. The human race has never been more unhappy than it is right now. Thousands of people are hungry, the slums of our large cities continue to grow, and crime is steadily increasing. Recent years have been marked by wars more savage and cruel than in any period of history. Assassinations have profoundly affected the history of our era, and student violence, riots, and broken homes dot our societal landscape.

Man needs God, but in his own wisdom is unable to find Him. Therefore, he will never experience real happiness until he abandons confidence in himself and looks to God for help. We will do our young people a great favor if we show them the record of man's failure.

HEDONISM LEADS TO FRUSTRATION

Having shown our youth that human wisdom fails to solve life's most serious problems, we must proceed to teach them the fallacy of the prevailing attitudes toward moral conduct. The philosophy of life they continually encounter may be expressed in the words, "If you enjoy it, then by all means do it."

The intellectual leaders of our institutions of learning generally believe that man is merely a machine, whose thoughts and emotions are nothing more than programmed reactions to heredity and psychological factors. They do not believe that any person is really responsible for his own conduct, and therefore they declare that everyone should make pleasure the goal of life, assuming that the end justifies the means. If other people are not hurt, who really cares? It's your life. The "future is sacrificed on the altar of the immediate," and the moment of fleeting happiness is achieved.

This attitude was expressed very candidly on a television talk show recently by a man who said that he had left his wife and two small children to live in a "common-law marriage" relationship with a 16-year-old girl. He declared that the statutory rape laws are ridiculous, and that if he and the girl were happy, no one had the right to stop them. He went on to say that if a person finds pleasure in homosexual activity, he should be able to practice it and still be accepted by society. After all, every person should be permitted to do whatever makes him happy.

Christian parents should not merely engage in the game of "ain't it awful" when they and their teens encounter this philosophy of life. They should question and discuss the validity of the assertion that pleasure should be the basic goal of life. They should consider questions like these: Are we really programmed creatures without moral responsibility? What would happen if everybody lived only for pleasure? What if we decided criminals should not be locked up because they can't help being what they are, and should not be denied the right to "do their thing"? Can we live for our own desires without hurting others? What about the rights of the wife and children of the man who is living with the 16-year-old girl?

A serious discussion in the light of the teachings of the Bible will help your teen to see the fallacy of this hedonistic philosophy. It will not be difficult to show the teen that one person's pleasure may be another's pain. In fact, he will readily see that a demented person might enjoy shooting people just as a man might enjoy hunting ducks. Now, if he has a right to find pleasure in whatever way he chooses, no one should stop him from shooting his fellowmen. It will not take long for our young people to understand that a society in which every person is free to seek pleasure in his own way would result in social and moral chaos.

UTILITARIANISM UNWORKABLE

Another humanistic approach to moral conduct which we must show to be fallacious is the system called "utilitarianism." This viewpoint also sets pleasure as the goal of life, but can be distinguished from hedonism in that it acknowledges the need for society to establish laws to protect the weak from the strong, the peaceful from the aggressive, the honest from the ruthless.

Furthermore, it contends that we must look for long-range pleasure rather than momentary thrills, and that we should seek the greatest good for the greatest number. This view of morals appears quite noble on the surface, and some young people with high ideals and genuine compassion may be fooled into thinking that it is a fine standard for the regulation of conduct. It would forbid certain social evils, but allow for a great deal of latitude in personal conduct. This philosophy of life has an emphasis that has great appeal to our youth, and it claims to put the needs of others first.

We have an obligation to show young people why this view of morals is wrong. In the first place, it is not biblical. God has given us definite guidelines for conduct as recorded in His Word.

Second, determining the greatest good for the greatest number leads to many serious problems. Who is going to make the final decision? One person may say that mentally retarded or physically deformed children are a burden to the majority and declare that the greatest good for the greatest number would be served if these unfortunates were put to death.

As you talk about this, ask your teen-ager how he would feel if he had a brother with a severe handicap and someone wanted to take him out for execution.

You can also point out that someone might decide that a certain racial or religious minority group ought to be eliminated. He might be able to present a strong case for the logical soundness of his plan by pointing out that most of these people are unemployed, uneducated, and living on government relief. Their removal would lighten everybody's tax load. These arguments, however, would not favorably impress most teen-agers. They instinctively sense that no minority group should be exterminated, and that a code of conduct which justifies grievous atrocities in the name of the general welfare cannot be pronounced acceptable.

THE NEW MORALITY

The most noble naturalistic approach to moral behavior is usually referred to as "the new morality" or "situation ethics." Many people do not understand what the "new morality" advocates are really saying. It is important that we do understand them so that we can show our young people why they are wrong.

The advocates of "situation ethics" often claim to believe in God, but say that we ought to set aside all laws, rules, and principles except for those which are necessary to maintain an orderly and safe society. They declare that our individual conduct should be regulated by the principle of love, and love alone.

The two leading exponents of the new morality, Bishop John A. T. Robinson and Professor Joseph Fletcher, while advocating a life marked by kindness and integrity, insist that we must not go to the Bible to find absolute principles, rules, or laws by which to regulate our conduct.

Dr. Robinson states, "For nothing can of itself always be labeled as 'wrong.' One cannot, for instance, start from the position that 'sex relations before marriage' or 'divorce' are wrong or sinful in themselves. They may be in 99 cases or even 100 cases out of 100, but they are not intrinsically so, for the only intrinsic evil is the lack of love." (*Honest to God*, Westminster Press, 1963.)

In the same book, he points out that a young man should decide whether or not he should have sexual relations with his girlfriend by asking, "How much do I love her?" He should not concern himself with the question, "Does the Bible say I shouldn't have intercourse until after I am married?"

Christian parents should know what men like Robinson and Fletcher are saying, and be able to discuss and refute their ideas intelligently. It is easy to understand why many young people are intrigued by this view of moral conduct. A young fellow and girl who are in love (or who think they are) can quite easily justify taking sexual liberties by affirming that they love each other very much.

In addition, situation ethics appeals to the sense of social justice, which is often strong in idealistic youth. It is difficult not to admire a Robin Hood who steals from the greedy rich to give to the poor who are being treated unjustly. In fact, situation ethics opens up all kinds of possibilities for illegal action to help the unfortunates in society, and offers an apparent means of justification of this behavior.

FALLACIES OF NEW MORALITY

The "new morality" theologians are to be repudiated for several reasons. First, their ideas are contrary to what the Bible teaches. The Scriptures declare that God is holy, and that He has established laws by which human conduct is to be regulated. Man's responsibility is to obey these laws, not change them, or pretend they don't exist.

A second flaw to be found in the teachings of the "new morality" people is that their system doesn't really work. The word "love" must be carefully defined if it is to be meaningful as a way to live. As soon as you become specific and start establishing principles or rules for love, you are doing the very thing that "situation ethics" advocates wish to avoid.

Not long ago a student in a large university murdered his girlfriend because he said he loved her so much he couldn't bear the thought of her continuing to live in this cruel world. Mothers have locked children in rooms in the name of love, saying that they might learn evil practices if they were to meet sinful people.

The fact of the matter is that humans can rationalize the word "love" to justify almost any kind of conduct they choose. "Love" not only can be but has been twisted to provide an excuse for nearly every kind of evil deed. Therefore, it must be defined in terms of the truth found only in the revelation of God if it is to become trustworthy as a guide.

Another reason the "new morality" ethics doesn't work out in practice is its failure to provide for human weakness. Its advocates say that one should never plan before time what he will do in a given situation. He must make his decision at the very moment he faces it. But to take this position is to ask emotional creatures to make a choice at the very instant the "adult" or reasoning factor is not operating very well.

People get themselves into trouble continually by compulsively buying items they cannot really afford. If they had decided in advance exactly what they would purchase, they would have spent their money far more wisely than they did. Certainly the same principle holds true when moral conduct is involved. A boy and girl alone in an automobile in a dark and secluded spot may be under a great deal of emotional pressure to do something they will regret. In this intimate situation they are not going to think through the so-called love principle very clearly, but an advance decision to obey the law of God will fortify them to act in a wise, moral, and beneficial manner.

It is well for us to remember and to point out to our teens that emotions have a way of distorting our powers of reason. Suppose that a young married woman who has been deserted by her husband has a sick child who cries all night. She becomes very weary and depressed. It might not be difficult for her to give in to an impulse to kill the baby and then commit suicide, thinking this to be the way of love for both of them. But if she has conditioned herself to live according to the standards set forth in the Bible and has a deep moral conviction that God forbids both murder and suicide, the chances of her yielding to the impulse of the moment will be relatively small.

In conclusion, let us remember that our young people, while sometimes inclined for a time to experiment with sin, really want to believe that they are worthwhile creatures with a purpose and eternal destiny. But they face problems that cry out for intelligent and honest answers. They cannot help but be impressed with the technological advances that are being made.

To deal with these influences, we parents must conduct ourselves as mature people who believe in God and love Him. We should engage our young people in discussion marked by a friendly spirit, an open attitude, and a willingness to let them say what is on their minds. In this manner, we can lead them to consider with us the biblical teaching on the subject at hand, and we can point out the weaknesses and flaws in the humanistic views they are encountering. This will help them to renew their pledge of faith in Christ and to follow a course of life consistent with this commitment, for it will provide acceptable criteria by which they can judge the many aspects of their lives.

The Bible tells us that God created the universe, and that man has been made in His image. It also explains the entrance of sin and death into that world which came from God's hand absolutely perfect. Then, too, only in the Scriptures can sinful human beings, who know they are guilty in the sight of the holy Maker and Judge of the universe, find the way of deliverance from the penalty and power of sin. Jesus Christ is the only way to God, and all who reject Him remain in spiritual blindness. Paul declared, "But the natural man receiveth not the things of the Spirit of God; for they are foolishness unto him, neither can he know them, because they are spiritually discerned" (1 Cor. 2:14).

How thankful we who know Christ should be for the fact that our eyes have been opened to mysteries the most brilliant but unsaved scholar cannot discern! Let us impress this truth upon our teens, helping them to see the emptiness of human wisdom and the fullness of a life lived for Christ.

3

PRIVATE DEVOTIONS—

Bible Reading and Prayer

PERHAPS nothing in the life of a Christian is more difficult to maintain than a satisfying time of private devotions. Those who are able to establish a daily schedule for family worship often find themselves unable to read the Bible for their own personal edification, and somehow they cannot pray without letting their minds wander.

The believer who has this difficulty will not enjoy the same inner strength and serenity that others do who are able to gain spiritual benefit through Bible reading and prayer. It is obvious that Christian parents who have not established a rich and significant fellowship with God will be poorly equipped to give spiritual guidance to their teens. Perhaps you need suggestions for your own private devotional life.

We have already hinted at the importance of private communion with God. A man may be well-adjusted and capable, and may have gained the respect of his peers, but he will exert little influence in directing others toward God, especially his own sons and daughters, if he is not in touch with the Lord through the Bible and prayer.

As parents, we must acknowledge that the regeneration and spiritual growth of our offspring is the work of the Holy Spirit, and that we must be totally dependent upon His ministry for their Christian development. However, we can teach our children the Bible, and we can set a good example by living in accordance with the Christian graces, attending church faithfully, and engaging in family devotions. And if our thought-life is pure and our prayer-life is vital, we can have more confidence that God will use us to bless our children.

If our lives are not right, God sees our hypocrisy, reads our most deeply hidden evil thoughts, and is grieved by them. We can thus be hindrances rather than helps in the spiritual development of our children. Besides, boys and girls are usually quite perceptive enough to tell whether or not parents really are walking with God.

Since personal devotions are so important, they should be made as much a part of life as washing one's face and brushing one's teeth. Therefore, fight the temptation to let other things usurp your time for Bible reading and prayer. Don't allow Satan to win the victory by keeping you from your quiet time. The self-discipline necessary in doing what you know is right will strengthen your will and make you a better person.

Even more important, the Lord will use this devotional period as a means of great spiritual blessing in your life. This time with God should become so much a part of you that you would feel abnormal if circumstances made it impossible for you to keep it. Only through listening to the Lord and speaking to Him on a regular basis will you gain the spiritual qualities necessary for you to fulfill your responsibilities as a Christian parent.

THE BIBLE READING

Daily reading of the Bible becomes a delightful experience when you go about it correctly. Here are several tips for successful and enjoyable reading of God's Word. First, don't read long sections of Scripture for your devotions. Although it's worthwhile to read the entire Bible through once a year, avoid using your quiet time for that. Read a brief passage, then allow yourself time to meditate on the meaning of the verses. Don't let yourself become distracted by puzzling words or phrases. Look for a thought to guide you through any trials and testings you may encounter. Find promises, and rejoice in them. Try to find ways to apply the Lord's commands. Remember, you are seeking a personal message from God that can help you to be a joyous, triumphant, and Christ-honoring believer throughout the day.

The effectiveness of a daily period of devotional Bible study has been demonstrated in many lives. A young man was converted while serving in the navy during World War II. He was assigned to a place of duty where he was unable to receive spiritual guidance from experienced Christians, but he made sure his soul received daily nourishment from God's Word. Whenever battle conditions permitted, he read a chapter of the Bible through three times at a sitting. Then he would close the Scriptures and write in his own words what he had read. He then would open his Bible again and compare what he had written to the words of Scripture to see how thoroughly he had comprehended them. He followed this by writing down what the passage meant for his daily life. Then he would lay out his handwritten papers as he knelt in prayer and asked the Lord to bring the truths to reality in his experience. Needless to say, this man made great spiritual progress.

Later, he served many years as a missionary and subsequently became the director of a highly respected mission board.

Not everyone can make his period of devotions as concentrated a time of Bible study as this young man did, but every believer should take a few minutes to read the Scriptures carefully for instruction and personal edification. The Bible is related to our lives, and its message can bring assurance of forgiveness, cleansing from sin, and strength to face trials and temptations.

The writer of Hebrews reminds us, "For the word of God is living, and powerful, and sharper than any two-edged sword, piercing even to the dividing asunder of soul and spirit, and of the joints and marrow, and is a discerner of the thoughts and intents of the heart" (Heb. 4:12). When we read the Bible with a sincere heart, its truths probe the innermost recesses of our being and bring our subconscious motives to light. But this is not all the Scriptures will do for us. After revealing to us our true condition, they show us how we can apply the healing medicine God has provided for our sin-sick souls.

THREE IMPORTANT RULES

Three important rules, if followed, will make your Bible reading a means of spiritual growth and increased knowledge. They are: (1) accept it as God's Word, (2) obey its precepts, (3) interpret it literally.

Accept It as God's Word

As a believer in the Lord Jesus, you are a member of God's family. This means the Bible is a message to you from your Heavenly Father. Remember, you are important to Him, and He is delighted when you read the Book in which He speaks to you. This realization should cause the Bible to play a vital role in your life. Devour it as you would a love letter. The unconverted person can only see it as a dull collection of historical narratives and teachings about religion, but the child of God finds it a source of unending comfort, strength, and joy. He accepts it as a personal message from the Lord.

You will find some of the passages you read difficult to understand. In fact, some of the Bible stories may even be hard to believe, and certain teachings you encounter may be contrary to everything you have always thought. Do not allow these difficulties to deter you from continuing to read the Scriptures for information and spiritual nourishment. Remember that your knowledge is limited and that the Bible is God's Word even when you don't understand it.

It is not essential that you immediately solve every problem you encounter in the Bible. Many of these difficulties will clear up as you grow spiritually. Avoid being taken up with factual questions or complex material which leads you away from devotional study. Some people like to become involved in discussing the Jewish calendar, genealogies, and many little details which are really quite insignificant. Such pursuits do not nourish your soul or lead you into a closer walk with God.

Paul warned believers against being overly concerned with debatable details and puzzling problems when he said, "But avoid foolish questions, and genealogies, and contentions, and strivings about the law; for they are unprofitable and vain" (Titus 3:9). Always keep in mind that your devotional time is intended to place you in communication with the Lord. He desires to speak to you through His Word so that you will mature spiritually.

Obey Its Precepts

The reading of the Scriptures as God's Word for your spiritual growth must be accompanied by obedience to its precepts. Unless you obey what the Bible says, your daily reading will not result in a transformed life. A spirit of submission to the will of God is an absolute imperative. You never will fully enjoy the blessedness of Christ nor become an effective Christian parent unless you decide you want to obey the Lord's directions. This should be the natural desire of every believer, for once he has received the new birth, he should possess a deep love for the Lord Jesus. Our Savior said, "If ye love Me, keep My commandments" (John 14:15).

As you read the Bible in your time of devotion, think of some practical ways you can apply its teachings to your life. Throughout the day, bring its thoughts to mind so that they become an integral part of your conscious life. When you do, the sins of the flesh and the temptations of the world will gradually lose their power, and the likeness of the Lord Jesus will begin to be reflected in your character and conduct. Your fellow workers and the members of your family will see in you an indefinable quality that will make them realize that your Christianity is for real.

Interpret It Literally
The third rule for a devotional reading of the Bible with real spiritual profit is to interpret it literally. This means that every passage should be taken to mean exactly what it says unless the context or the expression itself indicates otherwise. I am emphasizing this truth because so often people read the Bible and become discouraged when they can't explain a passage. They ask others or read commentaries for help, but do not receive it. They study books about the Bible, listen to a multitude of radio and television programs that are religious in nature, but become confused because of the wide divergence of views they encounter. They finally conclude that the Scriptures must be full of mysteries which can

be deciphered only by people who possess some kind of magical code.

It is not difficult to understand why such people despair of understanding the Bible. Some of the voices to which they are listening represent a wrong approach to the Scriptures or unsound methods of interpretation. Some Bible teachers, for example, are continually finding today's headlines in certain Old Testament passages. They twist the words of Scripture to fit the situation, and proclaim their so-called revelation with an air of confidence. Others devise strange teachings all their own, and declare that until they arrived on the scene no one in the Christian church really grasped the message of the Scriptures.

Do not allow such people to discourage you. Often they are guilty of reading their own thoughts into the Bible, and what they say does not really come from the Scriptures at all. If you will read the Word of God like any other authentic book, using accepted laws of grammar and logic, you will gain a good basic understanding of what it teaches. Rely upon the Holy Spirit, and use good common sense as you go about your study.

Let me again emphasize that it is unwise to become bogged down with a deep and involved study of difficult problems during your devotions. If you do, you will not accomplish the primary purpose of your quiet time—to receive a message from God for your daily life.

In summary, the reading of the Bible devotionally can become a life-transforming and delightful experience for you if you will approach it as God's Word given to you for spiritual nourishment, if you will obey its precepts, and if you will interpret it by the use of accepted laws of grammar and logic.

THE PRAYERS

The essential ingredient of one's devotional life is prayer, and the parent who does not intercede before the Throne of Grace for his children is failing them. Nothing you can do in behalf of your sons or daughters is more important than your prayers for them. When you fail in this Christian privilege you are ignoring God, the ultimate source of all life and spiritual power. You are really intimating that you do not need His help in regard to your children.

Earnest intercession has value beyond measure—both objectively and subjectively. In the first place, God does work when people pray. Second, teen-agers who know that their parents intercede for them before the Lord cannot help but be touched by this knowledge. Time and again young adults have testified to the value of their parents' prayers.

John Henry Strong, son of the well-known theologian Augustus Hopkins Strong, wrote, "When as a boy of 12, smitten with scarlet fever, my life was barely saved, was it not due to the pleadings of my mother, who as nurse and intercessor poured out her life almost unto death for me? When, grown to manhood, I once escaped being swept off my feet by fierce temptation just because I was too blind at the moment to see it, was it not because my godly father had daily prayed to God to guard his son, keep him pure, and save him whole for the Christian ministry?

"My parents' prayers were in front, behind, underneath and around everything I ever thought, did, or endured; and often I used to wonder what would befall me when I was deprived by death of the blessing of their prayers. Once, called to my mother's bedside, I found her in a coma and apparently near her end. As I stood there, I ventured to ask, 'Mother, if you should go to heaven before I do, could you help me from there?' She roused herself back into consciousness and with utmost decision answered, 'It would not be necessary.' That comforted me, for it showed me that if she were taken, God would provide other people and I should not be bereft. He has."

PREREQUISITES FOR EFFECTIVE PRAYER

Christian parent, if you really desire to be an effective intercessor, you must fulfill the following basic prerequisites. You must have a deep longing for holiness, desire a greater measure of compassion, and long for fellowship with God.

THE LONGING FOR HOLINESS

We adults often talk about the temptations young people face and warn them to abstain from evil. But what about our personal holiness? Among the unregenerate, many parents of teens are engaging in extramarital relationships, dishonest business dealings, excessive drinking, and other practices which make it impossible for them to admonish their sons and daughters.

Even among true believers, too many parents are far from being Christlike in character and conduct. The majority live a respectable life in the presence of others, and are not phony to the point that their children cannot respect them. But they are not walking with God in close fellowship, and their sons and daughters know it.

To find out what you really are, ask yourself the question, "What occupies my thinking when I am all alone?" Are your thoughts materialistic, selfish, tinged with envy, or sensual? If so, you should be concerned about your spiritual condition and realize that your prayers cannot be effective. The Psalmist declared, "If I regard iniquity in my heart, the Lord will not hear me" (Ps. 66:18). Every believer should cry out with the penitent David, "Create in me a clean heart, O God, and renew a right spirit within me" (Ps. 51:10).

Since your prayer-life cannot be effective without genuine godliness, ask the Lord to help you become more Christlike. Meditate upon the Savior's loveliness and character and conduct, and think about the depth of His love.

Remember, it is a law of life that we begin to resemble the people we admire and observe. This can be seen clearly in children adopted at an early age, for they often develop so many likenesses to their parents in the way they act that strangers can hardly believe they weren't born into the family.

This is also true in the realm of the spiritual, for the Apostle Paul declared, "But we all, with unveiled face beholding as in a mirror the glory of the Lord, are changed into the same image from glory to glory, even as by the Spirit of the Lord" (2 Cor. 3:18). How we need to desire earnestly that our lives manifest the purity, love, and truthfulness of our Savior! The way to grow in likeness to Him is by reading the New Testament, meditating upon His qualities as they are revealed there, and obeying His precepts.

Of course, this means that we will not only reflect upon the Lord Jesus during the brief periods of devotion, but that we will think about Him from time to time throughout the entire day. Yes, the longing for holiness is an absolute prerequisite for effective prayer. God cannot honor our petitions when our lives are dominated by selfishness and impurity, and when we are satisfied to remain in this condition.

DESIRE FOR COMPASSION

A productive prayer-life is also dependent upon a right attitude toward people. The Bible repeatedly enjoins us to love others even when they treat us badly, to have a forgiving spirit, and to be compassionate toward all. If we are indifferent to the spiritual, physical, and material needs of people around us, we are not on praying ground. We may offer lengthy prayers in which we utter beautiful words of devotion to Jesus Christ, but they will be unacceptable to God if we are so preoccupied with ourselves that we give no thought to anyone outside our own small circle.

Most people are not really hard-hearted to the extent that when they see a person writhing in pain, starving, or weeping, they do not have any feeling for him. However, people do have a way of insulating themselves from the sufferings of the masses who undergo severe pain, hunger, or sorrow. To do this is to evade our responsibility as Christians.

James, a brother of Jesus, declared, "Pure religion and undefiled before God and the Father is this: to visit the fatherless and widows in their affliction, and to keep oneself unspotted from the world.

"What doth it profit, my brethren, though a man say he hath faith, and have not works? Can faith save him? If a brother or sister be naked, and destitute of daily food, and one of you say unto them, Depart in peace, be ye warmed and filled; notwithstanding, ye give them not those things which are needful to the body, what doth it profit? Even so faith, if it hath not works, is dead, being alone. Yea, a man may say, Thou hast faith, and I have works; show me thy faith without thy works, and I will show thee my faith by my works. Thou believest that there is one God; thou doest well. The demons also believe, and tremble. But wilt thou know, O vain man, that faith without works is dead?" (James 1:27, 2:14-20).

We should keep in mind the fact that compassion

is the true manifestation of Christian love. Therefore, when we are unmoved or unconcerned about the needs of our fellowmen, we are sinning and do not really love God. The Apostle John declared, "If a man says, I love God, and hateth his brother, he is a liar; for he that loveth not his brother, whom he hath seen, how can he love God, whom he hath not seen? And this commandment have we from Him, that he who loveth God love his brother also" (1 John 4:20, 21).

You may wonder how to develop this compassion for others. Your own problems seem to occupy most of your time, and you find it impossible to be greatly concerned about the difficulties of people outside your family.

The first thing to do is to ask the Lord to give you a tender heart. Then begin to learn about the unpleasant situations in which many people find themselves. Take a good look at the ghettos where people live in dire poverty. Visit friends and acquaintances who are in the hospital. Call on a lonely relative, former neighbor, or acquaintance who is in a rest home. Try to enter into the circumstances of people you see by imagining yourself in their situation. Ask yourself, *How would I feel if I were in his shoes? What would I do?*

After you have begun to feel compassion for others, you'll be able to pray more unselfishly. Your intercessions will include more than just your immediate family. You'll find yourself praying for others too. When you do this, the Lord will honor your prayers. Moreover, your sons and daughters will be able to see that you are sincere, and that people are important to you.

YEARNING FOR HIS FELLOWSHIP

The third ingredient of effective prayer is a yearning for fellowship with God. This will be a natural consequence once you reach the point where you are deeply grateful for His grace, hate your sin, and really want to be pure and kind.

The Apostle John declared that his purpose in writing down the facts of Christ's life, death, and resurrection, along with many of Jesus' words, was "that ye also may have fellowship with us; and truly our fellowship is with the Father, and with His Son, Jesus Christ" (1 John 1:3). Fellowship with God! This means that we can communicate with Him, sharing with Him our joys and sorrows, our triumphs and disappointments, our hopes and fears, and our aspirations and burdens. Through faith in Christ, we have been brought into a vital union with God. He is now our Heavenly Father. Since this is true, we should have the same desire to talk to Him and listen to His voice as the child who wants to communicate with his parents.

Many years ago Dr. A. W. Tozer, speaking at Moody Church, Chicago, told of a Christian woman of several centuries ago who offered a prayer that went something like this: "Lord, I ask for three wounds. I do not shrink from the pain that may be involved. I am willing to suffer, if I can receive the wound of contrition, the wound of compassion, and the wound of a longing for God." This saintly woman realized that without these three qualities her testimony would have no real power and her prayers would be ineffective.

Mothers and fathers, are you willing to ask the Lord for these three godly characteristics? Remember, the future of your sons and daughters will be determined to a large extent by the kind of person you are. You set an example before them which will make an indelible impression, but even more important, the effectiveness of your intercessions will be determined to a great extent by your spiritual condition.

ELEMENTS OF EFFECTIVE PRAYER

The elements of an effective prayer are: (1) praise and thanksgiving, (2) petition, and (3) intercession. No one can prescribe the exact length for the prayers we offer in our devotions, but it is certain that we sin when we utter a few hasty words to God without giving them serious thought. Such praying is an insult to our Lord. Furthermore, our prayers should not be wholly occupied with requests for physical and material blessings for us and our loved ones. On the contrary, we are expected to offer praise and words of thanksgiving to our Lord, and to show concern about our spiritual needs as well as those relating to our physical well-being. Then, too, effective prayer must include unselfish intercession in behalf of others.

PRAISE AND THANKSGIVING

When you pray in private to God, begin by thanking Him for all His blessings. This should be natural, because it is the normal and polite thing to do in human relationships. If we meet someone who sent us a lovely card when we were ill, we usually begin by expressing our thanks to him. We don't carry on a lengthy conversation and then finally say, "Oh, by the way, I want to thank you for the card you sent me."

If you reflect for just a few moments, you will be able to find a host of reasons to give thanks to the Lord. The hymnwriter who exhorted us, "Count your many blessings, name them one by one," may have received the idea for these words from Psalm 40. David began counting all the mercies of God, but found he was unable to do so. He declared, "Many, O Lord, my God, are Thy wonderful works which Thou hast done, and Thy thoughts which are toward us; they cannot be reckoned up in order unto Thee. If I would declare and speak of them, they are more than can be numbered" (Ps. 40:5).

Every minister of the Gospel who has been close to people has had many occasions to marvel at the grateful spirit of a person in extremely difficult circumstances. From the mouths of people terminally ill, paralyzed, or handicapped have come beautiful words of gratitude to God for His goodness. The healthy person leaving the room of an invalid often declares that it was he, not the suffering one, who received the greatest blessing from the visit.

Real thankfulness arises from a redeemed heart. Therefore, when you spend time with the Lord, don't center your attention upon the things you would like to have, but focus upon all the Lord has done for you. Someone has said that we ought to thank God for:

Bread, in the measure He gives it.

Work, if the opportunity is still ours.

Friendship, with its cup ever sparkling, ever full.

Human love, that bright angel sent down to smooth every rough path and brighten every dark hour.

Home, sweet home.

Nature, her power to thrill or calm, her thunder-peal, her mother-touch, her divine instructiveness.

Music, a language sent as from some far-off sphere, bearing overtones like the beatings of an Immortal Heart, like the echoes of an Everlasting Sea.

Of course, we who know the Lord Jesus as our Savior would put at the head of the list *salvation,* for through God's grace we find deliverance from the penalty and power of sin and freedom from the fear of death.

Think of all the goodness and mercy God has

shown to you, and ask Him to make you more thankful than you have been. Gratitude promotes obedience and leads to the experience of the Lord's goodness. The Psalmist declared, "Whoso offereth praise glorifieth Me; and to him that ordereth his conduct aright will I show the salvation of God" (Ps. 50:23).

CONFESSION OF SIN

The second ingredient of effective private prayer is sincere confession of sin. A general sense of our own sinfulness and need for cleansing will almost inevitably follow a time of being overwhelmed with gratitude through reflecting upon God's goodness and mercy. We have said that a pure life is a prerequisite for effective prayer, but even when our conduct is marked by rectitude and integrity, we still fall far short of being all we should be. Every time we engage in private devotions, therefore, we should speak specifically to the Lord about our sins as the Holy Spirit brings them to our minds.

The Apostle John promised, "If we confess our sins, He is faithful and just to forgive us our sins, and to cleanse us from all unrighteousness" (1 John 1:9). Having acknowledged our sins, we must believe that they no longer are barriers to fellowship, and that God has removed them from our record. Confess, believe, and give thanks for His forgiving grace.

REQUESTS FOR SELF AND OTHERS

The third aspect of effective prayer is that of making our requests known to Him. Every Christian has spiritual problems, needs, and material requirements that must be met. The Lord desires that we place them before Him. Since our Savior taught His disciples to pray, "Give us this day our daily bread" (Matt. 6:11), we can be certain that God expects us to speak to Him about the whole range of our physical, material, and spiritual needs.

Effective prayer also includes unselfish intercession. We do not fully understand why, but it is a fact that God works when His people pray. Through intercessory prayer, hard hearts are made soft, miracles of deliverance are wrought, and the burdens of our fellowmen are made lighter. Dr. J. H. Jowett once said that he would rather teach one man to pray than 10 men to preach. Missionaries repeatedly ask for the prayers of God's people, and many of them can relate marvelous incidents which have taken place as the result of the intercessory ministry of Christians.

Be sensitive to the needs of people who form part of your daily round, and carefully evaluate the physical and spiritual needs of those for whom you have a particular responsibility. Be especially mindful of your young people, and remember that Paul prayed for the young man Timothy "night and day." Intercede for them earnestly as they encounter the complex pressures, temptations, and desires that make up their lives. God will honor your prayers, and you will be amazed as you see the answers come.

Remember that God is infinite in His power, wisdom, holiness, and love. He is so great and glorious that we cannot in any real sense comprehend Him. Yet through Jesus Christ, He has become "our Father who is in heaven." This means that though we must approach Him with reverence, we can also approach Him with confidence.

Dr. William Barclay, in his book *The Gospel of Matthew,* relates this account:

There is an old story which tells about a Roman Emperor who was enjoying a great victory celebration. This means that he had the privilege, which Rome gives to her great conquering generals, of marching his troops through the streets of

Rome, with all his captured trophies and his prisoners in his train. So the Emperor was on the march with his troops.

The streets were lined with cheering people. The tall legionnaires lined the streets' edges to keep the people in their places. At one point on the triumphal route was a little platform where the Empress and her family were sitting to watch the Emperor go by in all the pride of his triumph. On the platform with his mother was the Emperor's youngest son, still a little boy.

As the Emperor came near, the little boy jumped off the platform, burrowed though the crowd, tried to dodge between the legs of a legionary and run onto the road to meet his father's chariot. The guard stooped down, stopped him, swung him up in his arms, and said, "You can't do that, boy! Don't you know who that is in the chariot? That's the Emperor. You can't run out to his chariot."

The little lad laughed, "He may be your Emperor, but he's my father!"

That is exactly the way the Christian feels toward God. The might, the majesty, and the power are *the might, the majesty, and the power* of One whom Jesus Christ taught us to call *Our Father*.

Christian parents, don't neglect your private relationship with God. Let Him speak to you through the Scriptures, and commune with Him in prayer. Nothing will be a better investment of your time, or provide a more sound basis for the successful training of your children.

4

BIBLICAL PARENTHOOD—
The Do's and Don'ts

SOMETIMES it is interesting to listen in on a conversation at a church fellowship meeting, especially when adults begin discussing teen-agers and young people in general. Such remarks as these are common:

"Young people today just don't respect authority."

"If that James boy were my son, I would tell him he is not going to sit down at the table for another meal until he gets a haircut."

"These teen-agers today are getting by too easily, and have too much money to spend. Why, when I was their age. . . ."

"The other morning just before Sunday School, I walked by a car where four teen-agers were listening to some music on the radio, and you should have heard the horrible noise!"

"These young people today are so terribly critical that it scares me. They seem to think most adults are hypocrites, and some of their attitudes seem to be just plain un-American!"

All these statements are sure to gain affirmative responses, and provide enough material for a long "ain't it awful" game. I'm sure you have heard comments like these, and maybe you have found yourself agreeing wholeheartedly with the speakers, perhaps even chiming in with a few remarks of your own.

Such a discussion might also bring you some embarrassment because you have one or more teens in your own home, and they are wearing their hair too long or their skirts too short. You may have experienced chagrin because they often appear in public looking like they come from a poverty-stricken family. You may have felt completely frustrated after talking with them about certain religious and political issues on which you disagree. It is even possible that you are ashamed of the way they look and act, and that you envy those parents whose teen-agers conform to the standards of the adult world. You begin to wonder what you did wrong as you raised your children.

Now, it is always beneficial to review a situation to see where one could have done better. This may help to avoid the repetition of the same mistake. But when a parent is embarrassed and hurt by the conduct of his teen-ager, he sometimes reacts emotionally, saying or doing things which do not help the situation. Therefore, let me warn you against two frequently committed mistakes, and suggest two positive steps to take in regard to your relationship with your boy or girl.

DON'T GIVE UP THE SHIP

First, it is important that you don't feel utterly defeated because your teen-ager is causing you grief. You should not necessarily come to the conclusion that you have been a total failure as a parent. Don't let yourself assume that your rebellious teen is on the way to certain ruin.

If you are like most Christian parents, you really love your children, and your shortcomings in fulfilling your role do not stem from a lack of concern for them. You have been faithful in your marriage vows and are respectable citizens in the community. Think of the many homes around you in which children never receive even a semblance of Christian training, in which husbands and wives set a terrible example before their children by their lack of morals or by a casual attitude toward the marriage relationship.

Our Christian homes are different, however—at least most of them are. Of course, we have failed in some respects, and it would be well for us to acknowledge to our teens that we haven't been perfect parents. When they recall some wrong attitudes we manifested in time past or unwise disciplinary procedures we have used, we should admit our errors. But it is also important for us to recognize that many factors we couldn't control may have contributed significantly to the rebellious spirit of our teen-agers, even those in Christian families.

TODAY'S TEENS ARE PERCEPTIVE

One reason for not placing all the blame on yourself is that young people today are more perceptive than many of us were at their age. They see contradictions in the areas of religion and politics which we didn't always observe as clearly. As a result, we sometimes think of them as being irreverent or as lacking in patriotism, when in reality they are only being honest about the world as they see it. Remember, our young people are facing life's basic questions at a time when the inconsistencies of many of the religious and political positions of their parents are being recognized.

RELIGIOUS INCONSISTENCIES

Let us, for the sake of understanding, try to look at our churches and religious ideas from the standpoint of our young people, keeping in mind that the mood of the day is an utter abhorrence of hypocrisy. Our young people hear ministers talk about the power of prayer and the value of Bible study, but most of them observe that their parents seldom attend prayer meetings, never really study the Bible, and hardly ever engage in private prayer. Many of them have never heard mom or dad pray for them, and find it hard to discuss the Bible with their parents. They wonder why their folks don't practice what the minister preaches.

The teen-agers of today also question whether we really care about the needs of people the way we say we do. They know that Jesus was criticized by the religionists of His day for being kind to publicans and sinners, and they have been told that in the first-century church the majority of the members came from the poorest elements of society. But repeatedly they see our churches move out of depressed areas to build beautiful structures in communities where they will attract "nice people" from the middle- or upper-income brackets. They wonder what reason could be given for this seeming inconsistency. Do their parents really believe that God loves people in the slums as much as those who own beautiful homes and at least two cars? If they believe *God* does, why don't *they?*

Our teens also observe that many highly regarded people of the church talk in glowing terms about the Lord, and testify of how He has led them. But then they notice that these same people may say cruel and cutting things to those who interfere with their plans. They wonder how a genuinely spiritual person can be so unkind and hypocritical.

Our young people are often told that men and women who have never received Christ are on their way to a dismal eternity, but they observe that most Christians do not show up for church visitation. From the conversation of the adults they gather that sporting events and television programs are far more important than Christian service activities. They ask, "If telling people about Christ is so important, why isn't there more concern for this task among the adults?"

Pastors and other leaders in the church make no secret of their dislike for the way many young people look. Their distaste for the teens' music is obvious. But some never tell them why. Our teen-agers are looking for consistency, for honesty, and for logical answers to their questions. Too often they don't find them in church. It is up to us to engage in serious self-examination, to be ready with sensible answers, and to change our ways of thinking and living, if necessary, so that we may both help our teen-agers and strengthen the influence of the church.

POLITICAL-ECONOMIC INCONSISTENCIES

Our young people also have many questions about politics and economics. They see many inconsistencies in a society where extreme riches and dire poverty exist side by side. When they tell us that these things bother them, we should acknowledge the fact, and assure them that we are happy for their concern.

Of course, our youths do not possess a great deal of experience, and they tend to be idealistic. They are often extreme in their reactions, and their solutions to political and economic problems may be unrealistic. Yet we as Christian parents ought to recognize that some of the seeming irreverence and lack of patriotism they manifest is really the result of accurate perception as they look upon a complex situation. We ought to respect them for being willing to see things as they are and for being concerned.

All things considered, our teen-agers are living in

difficult days. Their faith is being tested on every hand, and they are being exposed to influences which contain a mingling of truth and error, and call for keen discernment. Since they are immature, they will make some mistakes. I am convinced, however, that the vast majority of those who have been brought up on the teachings of the Bible will modify many of their present positions, renew their commitment to Christ, and will either remain with or return to our churches. After they find themselves, many will be more zealous for Christ than ever before. They will be determined to make the church a greater influence for Christ than it ever has been.

DO BE HONEST

The way we react to the seeming lack of reverence and patriotism in a teen who is rebelling is very important, and the key word is honesty. Teen criticisms must be met with an attitude of openness and a willingness to face the truth. It is natural for parents to be defensive, thinking that their sons or daughters are rejecting them as persons or are simply determined to question everything that comes from adults. This is not true, however, for many young people today deeply love their parents and respect their views. Oh, they may think that we parents are a bit behind the times, but they expect that of us.

A common mistake we adults often make is to think that our children will lose respect for us if we admit that we were wrong in some of our views. If we as parents, upon being shown an error we have made, will honestly admit that our position was based upon prejudice or emotion rather than on a biblical or logical foundation, our teens will respect us more for our concession. They admire honesty.

Of course, they also want us to show our disapproval when we sincerely believe they are wrong in their views or conduct. They know that their ideas change from time to time, and that in a few years they will no longer hold some of the opinions they express so vehemently now. They have an inner admiration for adults who live godly lives and manifest genuine serenity. They are glad for every demonstration of spiritual reality in the lives of Christian adults.

They would be keenly disappointed in us as parents if we should vacillate in our basic beliefs. They have doubts and fears, and they need the security they gain when they see that the Christian faith really meets our needs. They are fortified when they are able to be sure that we have found Christ sufficient in every situation, for it raises their hopes that they can achieve the same kind of peace and satisfaction.

A young fellow in his late teens, who had dropped out of church and become associated with a wild crowd, recently came to his pastor's study. He told this servant of God that he had left the people with whom he had been drinking and living immorally and was going to begin attending church again. The minister expressed his joy at the news, then asked him if he would analyze why he was returning.

The young man replied, "I don't know for sure. I do know that I never really enjoyed myself, and that I always deeply appreciated my parents even though I argued with them. They were always open, and more than once my dad admitted that some of the points I raised were right. He and mother said they were sure they had been wrong in certain demands they had placed upon me when I was a small child. I also appreciated the fact that they never complained about how much grief I was bringing them. Instead, they treated me in a warm manner, even when my conduct didn't please them, and, though they didn't say much about it, I knew they were praying for me. I always found a great deal of comfort in knowing that they really believed in God and that nothing I had done could shake their confidence in Him."

We see in this young man's statement a genuine gratitude for the steadfast faith of his parents, and a great respect for them because of their honesty. No doubt that had much to do with his decision to return to the church.

Another teen-ager said that he stopped rebelling against the church at the time of his grandfather's death. The aged man had endured a long period of intense suffering and had become completely irrational. The boy's parents had prayed that the Lord would release the afflicted man from his suffering by taking him quickly, but he had lingered many months before he died.

On the day of the funeral, this son asked his father whether he had experienced any doubts about God's goodness during the time that Grandfather was suffering so much. The father had replied, "Yes, I had times of doubt. I don't know of anyone who can say he never has found it hard to believe. But I asked the Lord to give me grace, and reminded myself of the fact that I had committed my life to Him. I also decided that God knows much more than I do, and that I really have no right to question His ways. When I came to this point, the Holy Spirit gave me a deep inner peace, and I found that I could really believe the promise of Romans 8:28."

The father's honesty helped the teen immensely. That his father had experienced doubts but had come through them to victory was a tremendous factor in the boy's restoration.

Mothers and fathers, let's be honest. It is inevitable that our teens will see certain faults in us, and will recognize that some of our ideas may not be really based on the Bible. Let's admit our failings and acknowledge some of our pet theories aren't biblical. When we do this, our young people will admire us all the more, and we will be in a position to help them.

KING DAVID'S FAILURE TO BE HONEST

The story of David and Absalom is one of the saddest narratives in the Bible, and blame for the king's bitter grief can be placed at least in part upon his failure to be honest and open with his children. True, his multiple marriages and his affair with Bathsheba were contributing factors, but one cannot read 2 Samuel 13-18 without being dismayed at David's lack of parental involvement with his children.

This tendency of the king to neglect the training of his children is stated specifically in 1 Kings 1:6 in connection with Adonijah. We read, "And his father had never crossed him at any time by asking, 'Why have you done so?' " (NASB). This verse gives added credence to our interpretation of the story of David and Absalom.

The story begins with David's son Amnon, who raped a half sister named Tamar. What did the king do when the news reached him? As far as the record goes, nothing. The Scripture says simply that when the monarch "heard all these things, he was very angry" (2 Sam. 13:21, NASB).

David also knew that Absalom, full brother of Tamar, hated Amnon bitterly for violating his sister. But again the record indicates that the father never talked to his sons Amnon and Absalom about the situation. Most commentators deplore the fact that Absalom's anger continued to seethe for two years while his father apparently took no steps to remedy the situation. It appears that David practically had forgotten the incident, for when Absalom asked for permission to invite Amnon to a sheep-shearing party, he didn't recognize any danger signals.

Then, after Absalom had occasioned the death of

the brother he hated so deeply, he fled to Geshur. Again, David allowed three years to go by before he made any effort to communicate with his vengeful son.

The relationship between father and son worsened, and finally Absalom actually tried to take the kingdom from David. Then, when the insurrection failed and the young man had been killed, the heartbroken king of Israel wept and lamented, "O my son Absalom, my son, my son Absalom! Would God I had died for thee, O Absalom, my son, my son!" (2 Sam. 18:33).

How different all this might have been if David had spoken to Amnon, Tamar, and Absalom immediately after the act of incest had taken place. To the best of our knowlèdge, he never rebuked Amnon's unbridled lust. His sons and daughter must have known about his sin with Bathsheba, and it would have helped them if they could have heard from his own lips the confession of his failure to set a good example before them. How wonderful it would have been for him to read them his Psalms of confession (Psalms 32 and 51 in our Bibles). He could have assured Amnon of God's gracious forgiveness, and he could have warned Absalom of the danger and evil of holding a grudge.

DON'T MAKE THEM ANGRY

We are now ready to consider the second negative admonition; namely, "Don't make them angry." This is the basis of the exhortation given by the Apostle Paul when he said, "And, ye fathers, provoke not your children to wrath" (Eph. 6:4); and "Fathers, provoke not your children to anger, lest they be discouraged" (Col. 3:21). It is possible for parents to exasperate their sons and daughters so that they become embittered. This can be done in a number of ways: (1) by using a double standard,

(2) by showing a condescending attitude, (3) by being overprotective, and (4) by undue harshness.

USING A DOUBLE STANDARD

Parents sometimes make severe demands of their offspring while they themselves are undisciplined in their way of life. This causes the young person to feel wronged. A teen-ager who is "grounded" for a week because he told a lie will rebel inwardly if he knows that his parents often use deceit to further their own ends. The teen will not trust them, and in his heart he will question their love for him. Teens in a home where such a double standard is in effect may soon express their inner rebellion and frustration by smoking in secret, drinking, or worse still, by using hallucinating drugs.

People often like to point to young folks who have been brought up in a very strict atmosphere but are now living in a wild manner as proof that restraints and prohibitions are harmful. They say something like this: "If you make your children go to church and lay down rules for their conduct, they will rebel as soon as they are old enough to express themselves." This is a wrong conclusion. The fact that you establish regulations is not the real problem. Young people prefer to have some restraints placed upon them, and they recognize the need for certain prohibitions. But they are angered and frustrated when parents punish them for slight infractions of rules and principles they themselves flagrantly violate repeatedly.

MANIFESTING A CONDESCENDING ATTITUDE

Another parental practice that can infuriate young people is to present an attitude of condescension. Some mothers and fathers are always telling their teens what to do and say in every situation and what to believe about every subject. They give the young person the impression that they do not look upon him as capable of making any decisions or of coming up with any good ideas on his own. This can inflict great psychological harm on the teen. He is emerging from his childhood state into adulthood and senses his growing responsibility to think and act for himself. If you do not allow him this privilege, he may become angry, or worse still, lose the courage to make his own decisions and live his own life.

BEING OVERPROTECTIVE

Still another way parents can anger their sons and daughters to the point of exasperation is to be overly protective. A careful balance must be maintained between being too strict and too free because permissiveness and a completely carefree attitude on the part of mother and dad are also undesirable.

Young people want to have their parents forbid certain practices which are dangerous, but they resent being treated like small children. Adults must recognize that certain risks are involved in almost everything one does, and therefore they should not prohibit participation in sports or other activities just because some danger of injury is present. This also holds true in relation to learning to drive and obtaining a license. Parents should not forbid the young person to take the driver's training courses offered at school. Yes, your son or daughter might have an accident, but then, you may too.

We parents must also show confidence in our teen-agers with respect to their social lives. If a group of young people under the supervision of responsible and high-principled adults is going on an outing, we should not be so fearful of the possibility of improper boy-girl encounters that we refuse to let our teens attend. If we are that apprehensive about the moral conduct of our teen-agers, we are really indicating that we do not have confidence in the effectiveness of the training *we* gave them. Besides, we can't keep them home all the time, and our youth resent a doting and overprotective attitude.

There are times, however, when a prohibition is in order, and may actually be welcomed by the teen-ager. It reassures him that we still love him, and sometimes it gets him "off the hook." He may have had inner misgivings about carrying out a set of plans concocted by some group of his peers, but doesn't know how to wriggle out of them without losing face. In such a situation, the folks do him a great favor by saying, "No." Besides, teens are really glad that mom and dad are looking out for their moral and physical well-being.

We as parents can often make our prohibitions palatable to the teen-agers by discussing the circumstances openly with them. We don't always know when we are being overly protective, or when we are just exercising good common sense. An open and frank talk will usually lead to agreement. Even if the young person doesn't wholly concur with the decision, he will see some reasons for our stand. This will make him less resentful, and even cause him to respect us the more.

As an example of a situation in which we should be frank in discussing our stand, let us think of motorcycles. Ann Landers, the newspaper columnist, repeatedly declares that parents should not allow a son to own one, and should forbid their daughters from going for rides with boys who have them. She believes that the large number of serious accidents sustained on these two-wheeled vehicles justifies such a regulation. Statistics appear to be on her side, but many motorcycling enthusiasts question her judgment.

We should talk openly about matters like these with our young people. We should prepare ourselves for sessions during which we will discuss the pros and cons of riding on a motorcycle. This is also true regarding attendance at certain places of entertainment, or participation in specific activities in the community. Remember, our young people must know we care for them, and also must be assured of our confidence in them.

BY UNDUE HARSHNESS

The fourth pitfall parents must avoid if they are to obey Paul's admonition, "Fathers, provoke not your children to anger," is that of undue harshness. Sometimes a mother will become extremely upset over something a son or daughter says or does, and may make cutting remarks that inflict deep wounds. A father might become angry and use his superior physical strength to inflict punishment that borders on brutality. In a few instances, strong boys have become so enraged by the physical abuse of a father that they have fought back. The idea of a father and son fighting like a pair of tigers is revolting, and this sort of thing should never occur in a Christian home.

Parents must always avoid the use of sarcasm or any device that crushes their teen. The parent, for example, should never make statements like: "You are so stupid that I am ashamed of you." "You may think you look pretty with your new hair style and the clothing you bought, but I can tell you that you are just plain ugly." "It's easy to tell that you're going to be a failure in life." Then, too, public humiliation must be eschewed, for it is a form of cruelty that can deeply scar its victims.

It is also well to remember that any time the punishment exceeds in severity the seriousness of the offense, the teen-ager's sense of fair play will cause him to become angry and exasperated. Parents must pray that God will give them grace to be calm and reasonable whenever they deal with disobedience or wrong conduct of any kind. Undue harshness is dangerous, leading to total rejection or intense hatred.

DO BE A REAL PARENT

The Lord expects each of us to whom He has entrusted children to be a real parent in the full sense of that term. Paul warned fathers not to provoke their children to wrath, and then proceeded immediately to give positive instructions to which we must pay heed. He said, "Bring them up in the nurture and admonition of the Lord." This command contains three elements: (1) tender care, (2) loving discipline, and (3) careful instruction.

TENDER CARE

A quality that should mark all parental dealings with their children, whether they be infants or young people in their later teens, is tenderness. This is indicated by the verb translated "bring up" in Ephesians 6:4. Calvin renders it, "Let them be fondly cherished," and Dr. William Hendriksen phrases it, "rear them tenderly." (See William Hendriksen, *New Testament Commentary:* Ephesians, page 262, Baker, 1967.)

A young person should receive treatment in direct contrast to the kind that would provoke him to anger or plunge him into discouragement. Gentleness in parental dealing cannot be overemphasized. Though chicks may be hatched by the thousands in incubators and seem to do well without a mother or father, God made human beings—even teen-agers— with the basic need for love.

In today's busy world, many parents fail to manifest the tenderness they should toward their offspring. They do not take time to show an interest in the daily happenings of the child or teen-ager. They do not ask questions which proceed from a heart that really cares, and many young people have the feeling that their folks are not really much interested in their problems. A father and mother who will take the time necessary to show a genuine and tender concern will be of inestimable help to their teen-agers.

LOVING DISCIPLINE

Tender care necessarily involves discipline. Realizing this, Paul declared, "Provoke not your children to wrath, but bring them up in the *nurture* and *admonition* of the Lord" (Eph. 6:4). The word "nurture" in this verse carries the thought of chastening, but not essentially that of punishment. It means that we are to set rules and regulations, and include along with them a just program of penalties and rewards. Faithfulness to this admonition requires that we will be firm to punish when it is demanded, but always under the guidance of the love principles. The word "nurture" in this text has reference to that which we are to do *to* or *for* the young person as he is being prepared for his life as an adult.

CAREFUL INSTRUCTION

Paul also indicated that we must give our sons and daughters careful instruction. This is implied in Ephesians 6:4 by the word "admonition." We must communicate verbally with our teens, explaining our convictions and listening to their responses in an honest and open manner.

Of course love does not demand that we agree with them when they are wrong. On the contrary, we must speak strongly against sin, give warnings with fervor and real feeling, and speak pointedly in relation to errors in their thinking. We must not hold ourselves back in declaring the Lord's attitude toward all sin. We must convey to our sons and daughters the truth that God abhors evil. The best way this can be done is not by mere expressions of horror or dismay when somebody talks about immoral conduct, but through a definite communication of what the Bible has to say.

We parents are rearing our teens in a time when the value systems under which we have lived are undergoing careful examination. Young people today see the politico-economic world and its problems from a less nationalistic standpoint than we did a few years ago. They are examining the priorities we have set up in our churches, and have a tendency to think we are majoring on minor issues, while overlooking the important ones. Many of them are facing problems in the areas of religion and morals, and they want honest answers. Some of them are succumbing to the desire to be accepted by their non-Christian peers, and their conduct is a source of dismay to the adults who love them and observe them.

We parents must be very careful, however, how we react to our young people, especially when they displease us. We should not necessarily hide our heads in shame and blame ourselves when our teens show a rebellious spirit. Nothing is gained by this reaction, and it is really a form of self-pity.

True, we sometimes can recall serious mistakes we made in the past, and we should acknowledge them both to our teens and to the Lord. But, recognizing that many other factors may also be involved in disrupting the lives of our teen-agers, let us take a keen interest in them and try to undo as much as possible the errors of the past.

Then, avoiding all practices which move them to anger or a sense of frustration, let us pray for them earnestly, rear them tenderly, instruct them as thoroughly as we can, and share our deepest feelings with them. The Lord answers prayer, and works in a wonderful manner when we diligently apply the principles of His Word.

5

PARENT AND TEEN

MANY a frustrated parent has thrown up his hands in dismay, saying, "I can't understand today's teen-agers! I don't know how to communicate with them. I don't like the way they dress and I can't stand their music. Their actions are a puzzle to me. The only thing I can predict about them is that they are unpredictable!"

But teens are also troubled by their inability to get along with their parents. They wish they could sit down and talk things over, but all too often their attempts to express their feelings honestly are quickly ended by an angry outburst, which leaves everybody unhappy.

Many young people hesitate to give their opinion or discuss a problem because they are almost sure the result will be a lecture instead of a sympathetic ear and an understanding word. Therefore they "clam up" around their folks, only occasionally saying what they think and very seldom letting their feelings show. They don't ever really get to know their mom or dad, and their parents never find out their deepest thoughts and emotions.

Such a situation is unnecessary. But it is up to

the adults to do something about it. We can be of help to our youth, and they in turn can enrich our lives, if we learn how to communicate properly with them. The development of a deep interpersonal relationship may involve a number of changes in our attitudes, some of which we may not be eager to make. In fact, we will probably feel threatened by some of the demands placed upon us.

We must begin by facing the truth that many teens will become moral and spiritual derelicts unless we remove the barriers keeping us apart. All of our good advice will be completely ineffective unless these obstructions are torn away. In this chapter we will set forth a number of basic facts about human nature which every parent must understand if he is to fulfill his responsibility toward the teen-agers that are part of his life. The four propositions to be considered are: (1) people are complex beings, (2) we are conditioned by early influences, (3) we are continually acting out roles, and (4) we are in need of deep and significant communication with others.

WE ARE COMPLEX CREATURES

The human personality is extremely complex, making it difficult to understand ourselves or others. We act, speak, and feel the way we do for a variety of reasons, and often we are not even conscious of what they are. We do not always respond to external events in the same way, and these variations in our behavior are not easily explained. In fact, man is an extremely intricate being, whether considered from the standpoint of the theologian, the physician, or the psychologist.

MAN AS A PHYSICAL-SPIRITUAL BEING

First let us consider man as he relates to God. The Bible declares that he is composed of a tangible body and a non-material soul-spirit. It recognizes that man has physical urges, but in no way indicates that these desires are evil in themselves. It also portrays him as being made in the image of God, but certain Scripture passages declare that through sin man has lost his spiritual likeness to his Maker. For example, man in his natural state as a sinner does not really know himself or God, but this knowledge is restored when a person enters into a real relationship with Jesus Christ. Paul declares that believers "have put on the new self who is being renewed to a true knowledge according to the image of the One who created him" (Col. 3:10, NASB). Man in his original state was also righteous in relation to the universe and holy before God, but lost these qualities when he became a sinner. Paul, however, declares that they are restored in one who has been born again through faith in Christ, admonishing believers to "put on the new man, which after God is created in righteousness and true holiness" (Eph. 4:24).

The person who has entered into a real relationship with God, therefore, is in the process of having restored to him the spiritual qualities lost because of sin. In addition, he shares with all men the image of God in that he is a unique personality with a rational mind, emotions, and a will.

The Bible uses the term "heart" to denote several aspects of the inner man. This "heart" is the source of his emotional state, his intellectual activities, and his volitional acts. When referring to the human tendency to evil, the Word of God speaks of this aspect of man's nature as the "flesh." Furthermore, the Scriptures declare that every person is so self-centered and dominated by this "flesh" that he cannot perform deeds good enough to earn God's favor, no matter how good he tries to be. The prophet Isaiah declared, "But we are all as an unclean thing, and all our righteousnesses are as filthy rags; and we all do fade as a leaf, and our iniquities, like the wind, have taken us away" (Isa. 64:6).

The Scriptures further state that man's depravity is so complete that he doesn't really understand himself. Jeremiah put it this way: "The heart is deceitful above all things, and desperately wicked; who can know it?" (Jer. 17:9).

The Bible, however, does not indicate that man has no redeeming qualities, nor does it imply that everyone is totally dominated by selfish interests. It recognizes that some people possess certain admirable characteristics even though they are not believers, and indicates that the unsaved person will feel pangs of conscience when he does wrong and knows it. Many people who are not Christians struggle within themselves when they face the problem of right or wrong conduct, and perhaps no one is so thoroughly bad that friends and relatives would be unable to find something good about him.

When a person becomes a Christian and receives new life from God, he still faces a battle with his evil nature. The Apostle Paul, writing many years after his conversion, declared, "For that which I do I understand not; for what I would, that do I not; but what I hate, that do I. For the good that I would, I do not; but the evil which I would not, that I do" (Rom. 7:15, 19).

Paul was bewildered by the fact that he continually did the things he didn't want to do, and that he repeatedly failed to perform the duties he knew he should. This godly man, who gave us more revelation from God on the pages of the New Testament than any other, was unable to fathom the complexity of his own nature.

Even the most devout Christian is capable of falling into deep sin, though his devotion to Christ is so great that he would die as a martyr if necessary. Since we are such complicated creatures, the Christian life is not easy. We parents must recognize that a few pious pronouncements we utter will not be adequate to help our sons and daughters overcome the temptations, the trials, and the struggles they face day by day.

MAN AS A PHYSICAL-PSYCHOLOGICAL BEING

Physicians also recognize the complexity of man, for though they deal with the body and its functions, they know that many physical ailments are related to psychosomatic causes. They admit that no one today fully understands the relationship between the physical and the emotional. They are beginning to acknowledge the possibility that procedures like acupuncture, which cannot yet be scientifically validated, may have a certain amount of therapeutic value.

The field of psychology also confirms the complex nature of man by the very fact that it is divided into many schools of thought. The followers of Sigmund Freud, for example, theorize that everybody is influenced by unconscious instincts, such as the sex drives, which they call the "libido." They say that the neurotic person does not have the needs of sex and aggression fulfilled. They portray man as a machine programmed in his "unconscious" to react with conditioned responses. They do not hold an individual responsible for his conduct therefore, and do not believe the person who is mentally ill can really be cured. They seek only to help him, through psychoanalysis, to gain a measure of freedom from his inhibitions, which they see as the "blocks" that do not permit him to achieve the gratification of his basic instincts.

In direct contrast to the theories of Freud and his followers is the school of thought usually termed Reality Therapy. Men like Dr. O. Hobart Mowrer, Research Professor of Psychology at the University of Illinois, and Dr. William Glasser, a prominent

California psychiatrist, are extremely critical of psychoanalysis, which seeks to probe deeply the subconscious mind. They believe that the harm done in this procedure outweighs whatever good is accomplished, and contend that it is best to leave certain feelings buried. Instead of intense questioning about the past, they confront a "mentally ill" person with reality and show him his responsibility to make his conduct match his basic concepts of right and wrong. ("Mentally ill" is in quotes because these men do not believe that this is a correct diagnosis.) They are convinced that every person needs the self-respect and approval gained by doing right far more than the satisfaction of mere instinctive or biological impulses.

This is not a textbook on psychology, so we will not attempt a *scientific* evaluation of various psychological procedures. We have shown the contrast between the method of Freudians and of men like Mowrer and Glasser to illustrate that man is indeed a complex creature who must be treated with utmost care.

In trying to help our teen-agers, therefore, we must recognize that they are complicated entities. A few superficial questions will not uncover their most inward thoughts and deepest emotions. Their real self is a composite of everything they think and feel, love and hate, anticipate and dread, believe and disbelieve, esteem and reject.

What they appear to be on the outside is often not a picture of what they really are, for they wear "masks" just as we do. That teen-ager who is belligerent and argumentative may only be trying to cover up a deep sense of inadequacy. The girl who is conspicuous by the way she dresses may seem vain or flaunting, but in reality she may only be trying to compensate for a deep feeling of insecurity. Too often we do not understand our own actions, let alone those of others. Therefore, we must be careful not to make harsh judgments about any teen on the basis of his outward behavior. Instead, if we wish to establish a deep and helpful relationship with our sons and daughters, we must realize that human nature is extremely complex and that a hasty diagnosis on our part or simplistic answers to their serious questions can do irretrievable harm.

CONDITIONED BY EARLY INFLUENCES

The second proposition that must be recognized by every parent is this: *we are conditioned beings*. True, every normal person possesses the ability to reason and to make choices, but we are largely shaped by the input of our earliest years. Each of us, therefore, in many respects is a product of his past. The fact that many facets of our lives are not wholly within our control was stated by the Prophet Jeremiah when he said, "O Lord, I know that the way of man is not in himself; it is not in man that walketh to direct his steps" (Jer. 10:23).

From the very moment of birth, external influences make their impact upon a baby. As he grows, the attitudes, words, and actions of his parents are making lasting impressions. The manner in which he is treated in the first three years of his life very likely will determine whether he will grow up to be an individual with a sense of confidence and poise or a person who is anxious and self-deprecating.

This does not mean that one is not responsible for his conduct, nor are we to jump to the conclusion that nothing can be done for a person once he has passed these earliest years. A teen-ager may bear scars in his inner being that stem from his baby days, but he can change. He is not a machine.

But you will never help that young person by telling him that you are ashamed of him or by rebuking him. Simply demanding that he begin to improve will not bring about the change you are looking for.

If you have a teen in your family with problems that are beginning to appear quite serious, try to understand him and be patient. It took him as many years as he is old to become what he is at the present moment, and the mere unfeeling exercise of your role as an authority figure may do him more harm than good.

He *can* change, but he may not unless you show him love, try to understand him, help him to know himself, and then finally lead him into a pattern of responsible behavior. You can accomplish this only when you expend unselfishly a great deal of time and effort upon him.

WE ACT OUT ROLES

The third basic psychological truth we must understand as we relate to our teens is the fact that everyone engages in a certain amount of playacting. Dr. Eric Berne has written a popular book entitled *Games People Play,* in which he shows that we often act out a specific role or ego state as we interact with others. He and other psychologists who use the transactional analysis method point out that the human personality is made up of three "phenomenological realities" which may be called *Parent, Adult,* and *Child.* They say we often change from one state to another, sometimes behaving like a small child dominated by his feelings, at other times acting like a self-righteous and all-knowing parent, and at still other times living like a rational, logical, and self-controlled adult.

If we take time to study our own actions and reactions, we will be able to discern these qualities in ourselves. Sometimes we relate to other people as equals, having a sense of adequacy and self-sufficiency without a feeling of superiority. This is when we are acting as *Adults.* Occasionally, however, we may assume a protective, supportive, or superior stance in relation to others, giving advice or help in a manner which clearly reveals that we think of ourselves as stronger, wiser, or better than they. When we do this, we are playing the role of *Parent*. Then, too, almost all of us at some time or other feel inadequate and inferior in the presence of other people, or allow our emotions to take over to the extent that we whine, complain, or break out into tears as we declare our inability to do that which is expected of us. This is the *Child* role.

No one plays the same part all the time. We assume whatever role meets our needs in a particular situation. Ideally, we should always function as adults, neither forcing ourselves upon others as helper or provider nor demanding their assistance and support. Since we will discuss this more fully in a later chapter, it is sufficient at this time to say that mothers and fathers must avoid not only the extreme *Child* role but also the extreme *Parent* role.

For example, no father or mother will help his teen-ager by assuming the appearance of deep pain or speaking in a whining tone of voice when the teen says or does something that does not meet with parental approval. This is allowing the *Child* to come out, for you are really saying, "Please feel sorry for me." On the other hand, it is possible for you to overplay the part of *Parent* in order to compensate for your own feelings of inadequacy. Sometimes, for example, a father will pontificate on every subject that comes along with an air of absolute authority, or continually dominate the teen by being his helper in every situation.

Both of these stances are disastrous, for they do not promote a helpful relationship between parents and their children. The adult who sends out pity signals, playing the role of *Child*, will evoke an emotional and childish response from the teen. The father or mother who overplays his or her part as *Parent*, by being an expert on all subjects and the indispensable helper, will never allow the young person to grow up emotionally. If we as parents will become aware of the fact that all people wear masks and play games, we will avoid many mistakes.

WE MUST COMMUNICATE

Another basic truth we must understand if we are to be successful parents of teens is that communication is an indispensable factor in human relationships. This is exactly where many of us fail. Somehow we think that if we teach our children certain truths and punish them when they do wrong, they will almost automatically become well-adjusted, happy, and useful members of society. Yet it isn't working out that way. Many teens who come from fine Christian homes and good churches are having serious problems and don't know where to turn for help. They love us and need us, but somehow they do not feel free to talk with us. We must establish an open, honest, and intimate relationship with them if we are ever going to be of real assistance. We can best accomplish this by engaging them in conversation, beginning on a casual level and gradually progressing to a real sharing of our deepest feelings.

FACT AND EVENT CONVERSATION

The lowest plane of verbal interchange revolves around facts and events. At this level we talk about people, the things they say and do, and the happenings of the world around us. Parents and their teens may have a mutual interest in sports, community projects, church activities, national or international events, and it is possible to converse about such matters without getting into an area of disagreement.

Usually no one is threatened by this kind of conversation, and it promotes a friendly atmosphere in the home. Every parent should do his utmost to make such discussions pleasant, and should be careful to avoid the temptation to gossip or speak ill of a particular person who is not well-liked by the family. To speak degradingly of other people does not honor Christ, and will not help you gain the respect of your son or daughter.

The adult should control his feelings so that he does not let his *Child* come out in emotional outbursts. He must also be careful that he does not allow his inner *Parent* to overplay its role by sounding too much like a teacher or superior instead of someone who is just sharing equally in conversation. In addition, a friendly discussion on this level should not be used as an opportunity to inject derogatory remarks about other emotion-charged, controversial issues. Such statements will close the door to these friendly sessions, which can at least function as a doorway to more significant communication.

This level of conversation has only limited value, for it doesn't provide the opportunity for the person to reveal what is in his heart. One of our problems today is that, in most family circles, church groups, or neighborhood coffee klatches, people never get beyond this level. In such situations it is possible for each individual to hide his opinions and feelings, and try to come through as a sophisticated, self-composed, and happy person.

Real interpersonal relationships are never developed when people do not get beyond this plane of communication. John Powell in his book *Why Am I Afraid to Tell You Who I Am?* (Argus), makes the following comment:

"The whole group seems to gather to be lonely together. It is well summarized in the lyrics of Simon and Garfunkel's *Sounds of Silence:*
'And in the naked night I saw
Ten thousand people, maybe more,
People talking without speaking,

People hearing without listening,
People writing songs that voices never shared.
No one dared
Disturb the sounds of silence.' "

EXPRESSION OF IDEAS AND OPINIONS

The next level above "fact and event" conversation is that which includes the expression of opinions and ideas. As we relate to one another on this plane, we begin a process of mutual self-revelation. This is an important level of communicating with young people.

When our teen-agers tell us what they think about something, we must be careful how we react. If they suggest an opinion or declare a judgment with which we do not agree, we must not register shock or disapproval, nor immediately "cut them down" for their viewpoints. If we do, they may retreat to their shell where they think they are more safe, and no longer say what they think. They may either change the conversation, or in their efforts to please us, say exactly what they know we wish to hear. They may not be honest with us simply because they don't dare.

Another reaction a parent must avoid is that of becoming argumentative. If you sense that you are growing tense or your voice is gradually becoming louder and more high-pitched as you discuss opinions or ideas with your son or daughter, remind yourself that you are allowing the *Child* within you to take control. You are not acting as a mature adult should.

Take a moment to evaluate your emotions and determine what has gone wrong. If you are becoming angry, ask yourself why. Is it because you are afraid that the arguments of your son or daughter are more sound than yours? Are you hurt because an idea you held as absolute truth is in danger of being exploded? If you will stop and think, you will most likely decide that your emotional reaction stems from a lack of confidence in yourself. You are not sure you can prove your point or win the argument. This boils down to self-centeredness, and therefore is sin. Admit this to yourself, and let your *Adult* take over.

Also keep in mind a suggestion we made that you do not allow your inner *Parent* to come to the fore. You may find yourself becoming indignant and self-righteous, giving your son or daughter the idea that he or she should be ashamed of holding the opinions expressed.

If you display this attitude, your teen may react in a number of ways, none of which is good. First, he may simply bow to your authority and never learn to think for himself. Second, he may become discouraged and decide that he will never again express an opinion to you because it is too risky. Third, he may consider you to be a phony who is too proud or stubborn to accept any new ideas that come from the younger generation. He will then decide to tolerate you without ever looking to you for help.

Therefore, you must make the effort to be reasonable, kind, and respectful when talking with your teen-ager about his ideas, opinions, and judgments. Let him know that you are still learning, and that these discussions are profitable to you as well as to him. If you disagree with what he has said, be honest and express your view, but give the reasons in a quiet and reasonable manner. Both of you will gain from this kind of relationship.

THE RELATING OF FEELINGS

The highest level of communication involves the expression of one's emotions, and we are not fully relating with our teen-age sons and daughters until they share with us their deepest feelings. They have fears, doubts, hopes, phobias, guilt complexes, loves, and hates. When they tell us about these feelings, they are giving us an insight into their real selves. How we ought to value the occasions when they relate with us on this level! But when we do not respond properly, we are failing them, and may even do them definite harm. Five rules that every parent should follow are: (1) be interested, (2) be realistic, (3) be nonjudgmental, (4) be honest, and (5) be hopeful.

BE INTERESTED

The importance of showing interest in what your teen is saying about his emotions cannot be overemphasized. Most of us have experienced the hurt that comes when a person to whom we are talking appears somewhat bored with our conversation and shows that he has no interest in what we are saying. We experience inner pain when we see him glance at his watch occasionally, hear him interject irrelevant remarks, or observe him showing signs of impatience and irritability. It becomes obvious that such an individual is not going to give us very much help, for he isn't taking seriously a problem which is a great burden to us. Don't treat your teen-ager this way!

If you "brush off" a daughter who is tearfully telling you that someone rejected or misunderstood her, you are making a tremendous mistake. You may think of her experience and feelings as merely part of growing up, but she doesn't see it that way. If you only half listen and then say something like, "Just forget it," she will be deeply hurt and decide that you don't really care about her.

Try your best to listen with sincere interest, and enter into the feelings of your teen. React with sympathetic understanding. As Christians we have the responsibility of sharing the joys and sorrows of others, and this certainly includes those of our own children. Paul exhorted us, "Rejoice with them that do rejoice, and weep with them that weep" (Rom. 12:15). We must learn to identify with our teenager when he expresses any of his strongest feelings—fear, hope, love, or hate.

As parents we must set aside our own selfish interests and fully enter into the emotions of our sons and daughters. We will more likely be able to do this when we live in close fellowship with the Lord. Through prayer and the ministry of the Holy Spirit, we can overcome our self-centeredness and be real friends to our teens, as well as to all the people with whom we come in contact.

We do not fully relate to another person until we have learned to rejoice with him in a time of joy or weep with him in a time of sorrow. So much conversation and laughter among people is of an extremely superficial nature. This is illustrated in the story of a cleaning lady who had worked for a rich woman, and was asked if she had considered her now-deceased employer a close friend. When she said no, someone reminded her that they were often seen talking and laughing together. She replied, "We were just acquaintances, because we never shed any tears together. Folks have got to cry together before they are friends."

Remember, rule number one for a successful heart-to-heart encounter with your teen is to be interested in him and become involved with him.

BE REALISTIC

The second rule for establishing communication with young people is to be realistic. If we remember that our teens are human beings just like us and that they have the same problems we had when we were young, we will not react with expressions of horror or dismay when they tell us about their guilt feelings, fears, doubts, loves, or hates.

Circumstances are such that there is pressure upon them to depart to some extent from the moral codes they have learned from us. For example, a girl may feel deep guilt because she permitted herself to become engaged in heavy petting on her date, and she may want to confide in you. If she does, don't respond with a shocked exclamation like, "How could you do such a thing? You know I never taught you to be that kind of person!" Instead, remember that she is a flesh-and-blood human being who is under a great deal of social pressure, and that she possesses a fallen nature. Instead of acting horrified and bursting into a tirade of verbal abuse, breathe a prayer of thanks for the fact that she feels guilty, and then respond calmly. Let her know that you love her as much as you ever did and that God will forgive her. Then try to offer really helpful suggestions as you discuss her conduct on future occasions.

We should evidence this same calm and realistic attitude of maturity when a teen-ager talks to us about his religious doubts. Some fine young people cannot help but be impressed by the things they are reading and hearing as they continue their education. They wonder whether there really is a God who cares as they think of the sufferings of mankind and the injustices in society. They may wonder if the Bible is true after all, and have difficulty going to sleep at night because doubts about God, salvation, and life after death run through their minds.

If such a person comes to us to express these feelings, he does not need a rebuke. Instead, he should be given consideration, kindness, and a sympathetic ear. Let him express himself without interruption, and do not show a strong emotional response which will make him wish he had never told you about his doubts.

BE NONJUDGMENTAL

A third rule to follow if one is to enter into a rich interpersonal relationship with another is to be non-judgmental. By this I do not mean that you should adopt the philosophy that nothing is right or wrong in itself. Christians recognize that God has established moral standards through the Bible, and that they serve as guidelines for conduct.

If a teen-ager who has been taught God's Word does something wrong, he will know that he has sinned and will feel guilty about it. He will not need a reminder of this fact at the very moment he is experiencing deep emotional trauma. A severe warning or rebuke from you at this point will stop all effective communication. So will a strong remark like, "You feel this way because you have been listening to those good-for-nothing friends of yours and those stupid teachers who have no respect for God."

A pious pronouncement like, "You wouldn't feel this way if you were living in fellowship with the Lord" is also unnecessary and could be very harmful. The writer of Ecclesiastes said that there is "a time to keep silence, and a time to speak" (Eccl. 3:7), and in relation to teens we must recognize that on some occasions we should listen and respond without giving them a lecture or rebuke.

BE HONEST

The fourth rule we must observe for effective conversation with our teens is to be honest. If we in our youth experienced problems similar to theirs, we should admit it. If we went through periods of feeling guilty, we ought to let them know. When they see us as mature Christians and well-adjusted adults, they will be encouraged, realizing that they too can surmount their difficulties. In addition, they will become honest with us, which will provide even greater opportunities for us to help them.

Honesty does not require that we go into every detail as we admit our problems and weaknesses. If we went through a sordid experience, we need not tell them everything that happened. It does mean, however, that we will tear off the mask of sophistication and spiritual pretense that we so often wear. We will let them know that we are human and imperfect just as they are, and therefore we understand how they feel.

BE HOPEFUL

The fifth formula for a significant encounter with your son or daughter is an attitude of hopefulness. A young person should know that God forgives his every sin, understands his feelings, and will give him victory. You can help by showing him that you fully forgive and that you understand.

If you are living in fellowship with the Lord and know the presence of Christ as a reality in your life, you can relate your own experience to your teen, and give assurance that God will do the same for him. If he is discouraged because he is suffering from a deep inferiority complex, or if you can sense severe psychological problems, maintain an attitude of hopefulness, letting him know that he can be helped.

If the problem is of such a nature that it will require professional assistance, assure him that you will get help for him through a Christian psychologist or psychiatrist. You as a parent must continue to fulfill your role, however, even if you obtain the services of a professional person.

Show your teen-ager that you are interested, that you care, and that you understand. Be honest. Don't give up hope. Pray with him when he comes to you with problems. Your teen will discover that God does answer prayer, and he will gradually learn that through a personal walk with God he can find the strength and grace to live a happy and successful Christian life.

6

PARENTAL COUNSELING—
The Biblical Method

DURING the past two or three decades psychologists and psychiatrists have risen to a place of respect and admiration in the eyes of the general public. Many emotionally troubled people have experienced a measure of relief through psychotherapy or by attending counseling sessions coupled with medication and shock therapy. Anyone who reads current publications has encountered an increasing number of psychological terms like *ego, neurosis, psychosis, paranoia,* or *schizophrenia.* We are truly living in the age of the psychologist.

Many attitudes of our society are the result of the general acceptance of Freudian thought. The news media, for example, give the impression that most people who commit bizarre crimes are not really responsible for their acts, but either society drove them to it or they are mentally ill. That is why, in the wake of the assassinations of President John F. Kennedy, the Rev. Martin Luther King, and Senator Robert F. Kennedy, the editors and columnists of many newspapers and magazines did not blame Lee Harvey Oswald, James Earl Ray, or Sirhan Sirhan nearly as much as they did the entire populace.

It is common today to hear that criminals should not be punished, but treated by a psychiatrist instead. Followers of current psychological theories contend that if these people can see why they behave the way they do, they will correct their conduct. Then too, other writers, purporting to analyze the anti-social behavior of certain persistent lawbreakers, lay the blame on an overly strict "puritanical" atmosphere to which they were subjected at home or in church. Parents are warned against suppressing the behavior of their sons and daughters, for this is said to be a threat to their mental health.

Is it any wonder that some Christian fathers and mothers are confused and frightened today? They know that according to the Bible they are to instruct and discipline their children, but all this talk about the mental illnesses that result from a too strict home environment causes them to wonder what is right. Moreover, many of the newer books they read instruct them to be nondirective as they train their children; but when they study the Bible, they find it filled with exhortations and admonitions to both adults and children.

BIBLICAL VERSUS FREUDIAN PSYCHOLOGY

A true believer will regard the teachings of Scriptures above those of any mere human being, and therefore will weigh carefully the advice of many current books on child training. God's command to the mothers and fathers in Israel was, "And these words, which I command thee this day, shall be in thine heart; and thou shalt teach them diligently unto thy children, and shalt talk of them when thou sittest in thine house, and when thou walkest by the way, and when thou liest down, and when thou risest up. And thou shalt bind them for a sign upon thine hand, and they shall be as frontlets between thine eyes. And thou shalt write them upon the posts of thy house, and on thy gates" (Deut. 6:6-9).

Solomon, the man who received great wisdom from God, wrote, "Train up a child in the way he should go and, when he is old, he will not depart from it" (Prov. 22:6).

The Apostle Paul, as noted in an earlier chapter in this book, exhorted, "And, ye fathers, provoke not your children to wrath, but bring them up in the nurture and admonition of the Lord" (Eph. 6:4).

It should be immediately obvious that these passages do not advocate the nondirective method of child training as taught by Carl Rogers and others, for they give explicit command to parents to train their children. The Rogerians, however, claim that we must first help a person see his problem by simply listening to him, and then by probing into his past. The idea is that when the individual understands himself, he will be able to accept whatever flaws he may possess, eliminate his guilt feelings, and finally begin to enjoy life.

The parent who applies this technique listens to what his son or daughter says without ever responding with a word of authority, advice, or rebuke. But how can a Christian mother or father honestly follow this method? To do so is to deny that some deeds are right and others are wrong. It is to contend that everybody, even your teen, has the right to set his own standards and follow whatever pattern of conduct he thinks will give him happiness. Believers know, however, that a holy God has established an unchanging moral law, and that the Bible sets forth specific rules and regulations for life. They realize that it is their duty to teach their children what the Scriptures say, to insist upon obedience to God's law, and to exercise discipline when His commands are violated.

CONFLICTING VIEWS REGARDING SIN AND GUILT

A basic distinction between the teachings of the Bible and the views of Freudian psychology involves sin and guilt. Most so-called experts in the field of counseling proceed on the assumption that man is a highly complex animal who secures his greatest happiness when he is free from guilt feelings. They do not believe any person ever really does wrong.

Freudian psychologists give two reasons for their viewpoint. First, they claim that human beings are programmed almost completely by the circumstances and influences of their earliest years. They contend, therefore, that no one can really help being what he is or doing what he does. How can one hold a person responsible, they say, for that which happened to him when he was a child?

The second reason the Freudian psychologist denies human guilt is that he doesn't believe in the existence of a personal God. He reasons that there is no Supreme Being who is holy, righteous, and just, and that all guilt feelings are therefore purely subjective. As a result, he says that one should be generally free to do what he wants. He claims that people should remind themselves continually that the voice of conscience is only the reflection of an unfortunate childhood in an unhealthy atmosphere.

Psychology in the tradition of Freud speaks of three aspects of the human personality—the *id*, the *ego*, and the *superego*. Within the *ego*, the center of the personality, a struggle takes place between the base desires of the *id* and the loftier counterfeelings of the *superego*. This means that the sensual and instinctual urges of the *id* clash with the feelings of guilt, shame, and fear which arise in the *superego*.

Popular psychology declares that the way to find

happiness is to stifle the voice of conscience, recognizing that it only expresses an invalid sense of guilt. Once the individual understands that the real culprit robbing him of joy is the *supergo* or conscience, which has been conditioned arbitrarily since childhood, he will lose his guilt feelings and begin to find real pleasure in the freedom of being able to do whatever he desires.

This approach to mental health is contrary to the teachings of the Scriptures, for it denies the existence of a revealed moral standard. Therefore, a man unfaithful to his wife is *not* told by these psychologists that his infidelity is wrong and that he should change his conduct. Instead, he is given to understand that the only thing that really matters is whether or not his enjoyment is greater than his feelings of guilt. After all, his twinges of conscience are false anyway. This same lenient attitude prevails toward homosexuality and other forms of deviant behavior.

The outlook of the Bible toward the psychology of man is completely different. The Word of God acknowledges that human beings do indeed experience inner struggles, but it clearly teaches that peace is obtained by following the higher yearnings rather than the lower impulses. It labels the tendency toward evil the work of the "flesh," and commands that its suggestions are to be rejected. Paul declared, "Now the works of the flesh are manifest, which are these: adultery, fornication, uncleanness, lasciviousness, idolatry, sorcery, hatred, strife, jealousy, wrath, factions, seditions, heresies, envyings, murders, drunkenness, revelings, and the like; of which I tell you before, as I have also told you in time past, that they who do such things shall not inherit the kingdom of God. And they that are Christ's have crucified the flesh with the affections and lusts" (Gal. 5:19-21, 24).

The Lord Jesus also strongly demanded that we suppress our evil desires—the "elemental urges" which Freudians say must be satisfied. Our Savior said that even *thoughts* of evil are sin, and that every form of impurity, greed, or hatred must be dealt with in a radical manner. "Ye have heard that it was said by them of old, Thou shalt not commit adultery; but I say unto you that whosoever looketh on a woman to lust after her hath committed adultery with her already in his heart. And if thy right eye offend thee, pluck it out, and cast it from thee; for it is profitable for thee that one of thy members should perish, and not that thy whole body should be cast into hell. And if thy right hand offend thee, cut it off, and cast it from thee; for it is profitable for thee that one of thy members should perish, and not that thy whole body should be cast into hell" (Matt. 5:27-30).

The Bible allows no basis for excusing wicked thoughts, words, and actions as being perfectly natural or even necessary. It demands that we repudiate them as evil, drop them off as a foul thing, or kill them as if they were a poisonous serpent.

The Freudian therapists of whom we have been speaking would throw up their hands in dismay if they heard a Christian parent tell his teen-ager that his sinful behavior must be stopped immediately. He would predict that this young person will become the victim of deep guilt complexes, and that these will rob him of every chance for future happiness.

Do not be frightened by such assertions! God's Word is a sure guide, and human experience through thousands of years of history has revealed the truthfulness of the biblical assertions that sin pays bitter wages. Moses said to Israel, ". . . and be sure your sin will find you out" (Num. 32:23). Paul declared, "Be not deceived, God is not mocked, for whatever a man soweth, that shall he also reap. For he that soweth to his flesh shall of the flesh reap corruption; but he that soweth to the Spirit shall of the Spirit reap life everlasting" (Gal. 6:7, 8).

If you really love your teen-ager, do not hesitate to call evil conduct sin, and to point out to him that no one ever breaks God's laws without receiving just punishment.

CONSCIENCE VERSUS INSTINCT

The Christian attitude toward conscience is also opposed to that advocated by many contemporary spokesmen. The Bible teaches that the voice of conscience is a warning light which should be heeded, but most secular psychotherapists merely consider it a nuisance which should be silenced. The Freudian says that to be happy one must overcome all feelings of guilt and be able to yield to elemental urges without being torn by remorse.

The Christian, on the other hand, says that this procedure doesn't make any more sense than would smashing the dashboard of the car when the flashing red light indicates that the oil pressure is low. The intelligent reaction to the warning signal is to coast into a gasoline station and add the needed oil. When conscience speaks, we should listen to its warning, and make an adjustment in our behavior.

Of course, sometimes the red light malfunctions. One's conscience can be "weak" or misguided. But unless and until such a conscience is enlightened, one must heed it or stand self-condemned.

The Apostle Peter spoke of the value of a good conscience when he said, "Having a good conscience, that, whereas they speak evil of you, as of evildoers, they may be ashamed that falsely accuse your good manner of life in Christ" (1 Peter 3:16).

In this verse Peter is telling us that we achieve a "good conscience" by good behavior. When people revile us and persecute us because of our commendable conduct rather than that which is reprehensible, we sense a real satisfaction.

On the other hand, there are people whom Paul

describes as "having their conscience seared with a hot iron" (1 Tim. 4:2). This is the result of deliberately ignoring the red light on the dashboard. When a person repeatedly disregards the warnings of conscience, it becomes dull, calloused, and, for all practical purposes, dead. Paul looked upon this condition as most undesirable, for he placed a great deal of emphasis upon our being sensitive to this inner voice. For example, he declared in his discussion of Christian liberty that whenever a believer is in doubt about the rightness or wrongness of a practice, he simply should not do it. "And he that doubteth is condemned if he eat, because he eateth not of faith; for whatever is not of faith is sin" (Rom. 14:23). Never, never is the voice of conscience to be ignored!

It is encouraging to note that many prominent men in the fields of psychology and psychiatry have departed from the teachings of Freud, and have moved to a position closer to that which is set forth in the Bible. One of these men is Dr. O. Hobart Mowrer, Research Professor of Psychology at the University of Illinois.

Mowrer does not write from the presuppositions of evangelical Christianity, but he shares with believers the conviction that real self-acceptance and lasting satisfaction can come only to those who have a good conscience. He also declares that this happiness can be attained through proper behavior. He looks upon human beings as imperfect, but sees many of them as decent, morally good people. He declares that no one is able to accept himself and respect himself if he denies his guilt, suppresses his higher inclinations, and disregards conscience. He says that a person must acknowledge that his immoral or unethical practices are evil, admit his responsibility to change, and view his guilt as real, not as a mere complex. In an article "Sin, the Lesser of Two Evils" in the May 1960 issue of *The American Psychologist,* Mowrer wrote:

This is the paradox which we have not at all understood and which is the very crux of the problem. Just so long as a person lives under the shadow of real, unacknowledged, and unexpiated guilt, he cannot (if he has any character at all) "accept himself"; and all our efforts to reassure and accept him will avail nothing. He will continue to hate himself and to suffer the inevitable consequences of self-hatred. But the moment he (with or without assistance) begins to accept his guilt and his sinfulness, the possibility of radical reformation opens up; and with this, the individual may legitimately, though not without pain and effort, pass from deep, pervasive self-rejection and self-torture to a new freedom of self-respect and peace.

Dr. William Glasser, a prominent California psychiatrist, who served as a regular consultant at the Ventura School for Girls of the California Youth Authority, and also at the Los Angeles Orthopedic Hospital, came to the same conclusions as Dr. Mowrer. He states that the real human needs are not *sex* and *aggression,* as claimed by the followers of Freud, but *relatedness* and *respect*. He proceeds to declare that we can achieve a proper relationship with others and a sense of personal worth only when we do what is "realistic, responsible, and right." He continues in his book *Reality Therapy*):

To be worthwhile, we must maintain a satisfactory standard of behavior. To do so we must learn to correct ourselves when we do wrong and to credit ourselves when we do right. If we do not evaluate our own behavior, or, having evaluated it, if we do not act to improve our conduct where it is below our standards, we will not fulfill our needs to be worthwhile and will suffer as acutely as when we fail to love or to be loved. Morals, standards, values, or right and wrong behavior are all intimately related to the fulfillment of our needs for self-worth and are a necessary part of Reality Therapy.

Dr. Mowrer also emphasizes the need for people to obey the voice of conscience and follow the higher inclinations when in his foreword to Dr. Glasser's book he writes:

Conventional psychiatry and clinical psychology assume that neurosis arises because the afflicted individual's moral standards are unrealistically high, that he has not been "bad" but *too good,* and that the therapeutic task is, specifically, to counteract and neutralize conscience, "soften" the demands of a presumably too severe superego, and thus free the person from inhibitions and "blocks" which stand in the way of normal gratification of his "instinct." The purview of reality therapy is, again, very different; namely, that human beings get into emotional binds, not because their standards are too high, but because their performance has been, and is, too low. As Walter Huston Clark has neatly put it, "The objective of this (radically non-Freudian) type of therapy is not to lower the aim, but to increase the accomplishment." Freud held that psychological disorders arise when there has been a "cultural interference with the instinctual, *biological* needs of the individual," whereas Glasser and others are now holding that the problem is rather an incapacity or failing at the interpersonal, *social* level of human functioning.

The successes of the kind of treatment prescribed by Mowrer, Glasser, and others have been amazing. They come as a striking contrast to the failures of traditional psychotherapy. Glasser, working with girls who were acknowledged to be hardened socio-paths, was able to return 80 percent of them back into society with no repetition of the previous criminal and anti-social behavior. Experience shows that less than five percent would have made this kind of recovery under the older and more traditional forms of treatment.

Dr. G. L. Harrington, another advocate of the reality therapy school, took over the responsibility for the psychiatric treatment of 210 male patients in a V.A. hospital in Los Angeles. The men on this ward had reached the point of no return. Most were almost completely unable to function normally. The average release per year to make an effort at a return to life on the outside had been two until Harrington took over, but in his first year he was able to discharge 75 men back into the stream of human life and normal activity. He predicted that in the following year 200 would be released, bringing about almost 100 percent success in a period of two years.

Now, what does all of this mean to Christian parents of teen-agers? A great deal, I believe. It is another indication of the truthfulness of the Bible. It underscores the correctness of the method of child-raising the Word of God enjoins upon all fathers and mothers. These reports should confirm your belief that you must teach your sons and daughters to live responsibly in accordance with God's moral laws.

As a Christian parent who believes the Bible, you have a decided advantage over men like Mowrer and Glasser in counseling your teens. They do not accept the Scriptures as authoritative, nor do they profess to believe in the forgiveness that comes through faith in Jesus Christ. Therefore, they are vague in their answers when someone presses them to give a clear definition of right and wrong, or asks them to explain just what they mean by reality.

They admit that their approach is on a practical level, and that one might find their assertions philosophically inadequate. Christian parents have a perfect guidebook in the Bible, and can show their teens how to gain the assurance of complete forgiveness through faith in Christ. This will meet a deep need in their lives, and will inspire in them a feeling of hope that they could not obtain from the most kind and sympathetic non-Christian counselor.

TECHNIQUES FOR EFFECTIVE COUNSELING

If you as a parent know what you believe and why, if you are living in fellowship with the Lord, and if you truly love your sons and daughters, you can be of tremendous assistance to them. You will even be able to help them when they have emotional problems. In unusual cases, however, it may be necessary for you to send them for professional counseling.

INVOLVEMENT

As the first principle for effective parental counseling, developing a real involvement with the teen-ager is an absolute necessity. Without it, you will never be able to secure his confidence and help him through the rough places. You must take a keen interest in him. If you are to be truly helpful, however, it is mandatory for you to establish a genuine relationship with your young person without becoming overly sympathetic.

In the previous chapter, we discussed the need of talking with our teens on three levels—fact, opinion, and feeling. We said that the most significant conversation is one in which we express openly to one another our deepest emotions. This calls for absolute honesty and a manifestation of genuine love. A teen-ager must be convinced that we possess these qualities in relation to him, or he will refuse to open up to us.

It certainly shouldn't be difficult for us to take a deep interest in our own sons and daughters. Strangely enough, however, some mothers and fathers are so taken up with their own activities and interests that they give little serious consideration to their God-given duties as parents—in fact, they try to avoid them. This is a grievous sin, and we who know the Lord should realize the solemnity of our responsibility toward the children we have brought into the world. We must remember that all of us have an eternal destiny, and that in relation to our children as well as in all other areas of life we have an obligation to get our priorities in the right order.

PRACTICAL GUIDELINES

On the practical level, how do we go about gaining the confidence of our teens? Assuming that we are ready to be honest and that we are genuinely interested in them, one way we can achieve rapport with them is through asking the right questions. We should inquire what they are doing now, and what they hope to do in the future. Then we must build our conversation around their present activities and plans. This lets our young people know that we have confidence in them, and that we expect them to have a worthwhile future.

Though the highest level of conversation involves the feelings, our sharing of emotional experiences must lead back to a discussion of actual behavior. We must show our teens what responsible living actually is. We must firmly insist that good feelings flow from good conduct, and that the way to overcome discouragement, inferiority complexes, and depression is through a change in performance.

The Bible clearly teaches this principle. It is precisely what the Lord declared to Cain, who was deeply disturbed and filled with hatred for his brother Abel. Here is the record: "And in process of time it came to pass, that Cain brought of the fruit of the ground an offering unto the Lord. And Abel, he also brought of the firstlings of his flock and of the fat thereof. And the Lord had respect unto Abel and to his offering; but unto Cain and to his offering He had no respect. And Cain was very angry, and his countenance fell. And the Lord said unto Cain, Why art thou angry? And why is thy countenance fallen? If thou doest well, shalt thou not be accepted? And if thou doest not well, sin lieth at the door" (Gen. 4:3-7).

God told Cain, "If you do what is right, won't you be accepted?" If he would only begin to obey his Maker, and rid his heart of hatred, and offer the kind of sacrifice that had been prescribed, he would find joy and happiness. This principle of God is always true: *Do what is right and good, and good feelings will follow.*

KINDNESS AND TOUGHNESS

When you counsel with your teen, be sure he knows that you accept him as he is. Impress him with your kindness and genuine love. Assure him by your attitude that you do not reject him as a person, and acknowledge that some of his problems may stem from factors over which he has no control. Make certain he realizes that God forgives completely, and that you do too. Let him know that you have confidence in him, and that you believe he will become a fine and worthwhile person.

Yet you must be on guard against promoting self-pity, and make certain that you do not let him feel you are unconcerned about his irresponsible conduct. Carefully avoid the pitfall of becoming overly sympathetic or allowing him to get the idea that he isn't responsible for his wrongdoings.

The following advice of Dr. Glasser, though not

directed specifically to parents, is certainly applicable:

> The therapist who accepts excuses, ignores reality, or allows the patient to blame his present unhappiness on a parent or on an emotional disturbance can usually make his patient feel good temporarily at the price of evading responsibility. He is only giving the patient "psychiatric kicks," which are no different from the brief kicks he may have obtained from alcohol, pills, or sympathetic friends before consulting the psychiatrist. When they fade, as they soon must, the patient with good reason becomes disillusioned with psychiatry.

Plausible as it may seem, we must never delude ourselves into wrongly concluding that unhappiness led to the patient's behavior, that a delinquent child broke the law because he was miserable, and therefore our job is to make him happy. He broke the law not because he was angry or bored, but because he was irresponsible. The unhappiness is not a cause but a companion to this irresponsible behavior.

Is anything gained by giving in to an irresponsible 16-year-old boy who says he must have a car to be happy? A host of parents have learned through bitter experience that one cannot purchase happiness for an irresponsible child. A car merely allows the boy to extend the scope and magnitude of his irresponsibility and gives him some brief moments of joy before his pattern deteriorates further.

A girl who makes herself and her parents miserable because they won't allow her to leave high school to get married usually finds only brief pleasure when her parents bow to her pressure. Among the most unhappy people in our society are young, divorced mothers with two or three children who were too impatient to wait for emotional maturity before marriage. from *Reality Therapy*.

The parent must never accept from his young person excuses for bad behavior which place the blame on a teacher, mother and father, or society in general. He must always insist that the teen is to live responsibly now, and that if he does what is right, he will begin to feel better.

A daughter doing poorly in school and causing discipline problems may put on a scene in the home when a request she makes is refused. Between sobs she may say, "I am terribly unhappy, and it is all your fault. That's why I act the way I do. If you would buy me a new wardrobe and let me stay out later, I would become more happy and start doing better."

If you are fooled by her promise or give in because of a feeling of sympathy, you will be making a serious mistake. Be firm enough to say no. Remember, you will not alienate your daughter permanently by insisting that she keep the rules you have established. Actually, her tears and pleas are means by which she is testing the firmness of your resolve and the depth of your love. She will really respect you for not giving in and will interpret your determined stand as a sign that you love her and consider her a worthwhile person.

Some teens will waste an entire evening talking on the telephone or watching TV when they know they ought to be doing their homework. The parent has the duty to forbid the telephone and television, and to demand that the studies be done first. In response, the teen may run through any number of reactions. She may plead, promise, cry, threaten, or even throw a temper tantrum. But if she gets her own way, she will go to school the next day unprepared, and be embarrassed in the classroom. At that time, she will blame her parents for not disciplining her properly, and may be well on the road toward repeated failures for which she will hold others responsible—never herself.

Again turning to Dr. Glasser, let us note this significant statement:

> Parents who are willing to suffer the pain of the child's intense anger by firmly holding him to the responsible course are teaching him a lesson that will help all his life. Parents who do not do so are setting that pattern for future irresponsibility which prevents the child from fulfilling the need to feel worthwhile. *(Reality Therapy.)*

A BIBLICAL EXAMPLE

The story of Eli provides a biblical example of a father who did not obey God's directions regarding the discipline of his children. (See 1 Samuel 2:12–4:11.) When Eli is introduced to us, he is an aged man serving in the dual capacity of political leader and priest. Apparently he was a good man, faithful in the performance of his duties. One cannot help but be impressed with his kindness toward Samuel, even though he knew this lad would displace his sons in the leadership of the nation. But he was too soft in the way he treated his own boys. We are told that they were extremely wicked—"worthless men" whose scandalous conduct brought disgrace to the office of priesthood.

Perhaps Eli was so busy as judge and priest that he paid very little attention to his sons. At any rate, when he finally rebuked his sons, he was far too late and his words were far too weak. The Scripture states, "Now Eli was very old, and heard all that his sons did unto all Israel, and how they lay with the women who assembled at the door of the tabernacle of the congregation. And he said unto them,

Why do ye such things? For I hear of your evil dealings by all this people. Nay, my sons; for it is no good report that I hear: ye make the Lord's people to transgress. If one man sin against another, the judge shall judge him; but if a man sin against the Lord, who shall mediate for him? Notwithstanding, they hearkened not unto the voice of their father" (1 Sam. 2:22-25).

Dr. Jay Adams, in his book *Competent to Counsel*, points out that Eli made a serious mistake when he began his words of rebuke with the question, "Why?" Even if he asked it rhetorically, not expecting an answer, he showed a weakness which may indicate what the problem had been all along. He should have confronted his sons with their sins, told them that he knew exactly what they were doing and that their conduct was wrong. He should have warned them that if they did not stop these practices immediately, they would be unable to serve in their capacity as priests any longer. If they would not listen, he should have ordered other men to enforce his prohibitions. He had waited so long, however, that his sons had confirmed themselves in the pathway of disobedience. He had not taken positive measures during their youth.

BIBLICAL TEACHING ABOUT RESPONSIBILITY

The Bible definitely holds people responsible for their individual conduct. We recognize, of course, that in our sin-cursed world some babies are born mentally retarded or brain-damaged, and that tumors or other organic problems sometimes cause people to act irrationally. In such cases we simply trust the Lord's infinite wisdom, love, and holiness, and are assured that He will do what is right. We exercise the same implicit faith in God as we contemplate His judgment of people who have the ability to reason and make choices, but spend their entire lives in very unfortunate circumstances. The Lord knows the exact degree of light and privilege each person has experienced, and He will do what is right. We find great comfort in these assurances. Nevertheless, we cannot and must not minimize the fact of human responsibility.

Our young people today sometimes act as though they have been done a terrible wrong by their parents if they cannot have everything they want. They give the impression that their folks had no right to bring them into a world where everything is not perfect. We admit that many children are growing up in misery and poverty, and live in homes where they are not shown even a little love. We realize that many young people have died in wars for which they were not responsible. Many people die because of the negligence of others. A driver may fail to observe a stop sign, a doctor may make a mistake in diagnosis, or a pharmacist may inadvertently bottle the wrong medicine. That the innocent sometimes suffer and die because of what others do is a tragic fact of human existence. But in spite of all that, it is still true that every normal person is responsible for his conduct.

The prophet Ezekiel, living with the Jewish exiles in the land of Babylon, found that many of his countrymen were bitter and cynical. They thought God had failed them, and wickedly quoted a proverb, "The fathers have eaten sour grapes, and the children's teeth are set on edge" (Ezek. 18:2). By this, they were saying that their misfortune was punishment for the sins of their forefathers.

By inspiration of God, however, Ezekiel showed them to be wrong. He rebuked their self-pitying attitude, and declared the truth that every individual is responsible for his own sins.

A little later in the same passage the prophet said, "The soul that sinneth, it shall die. The son shall not bear the iniquity of the father, neither shall the father bear the iniquity of the son; the righteousness of the righteous shall be upon him, and the wickedness of the wicked shall be upon him" (Ezek. 18:20).

As Christian parents, let's try to demonstrate to our sons and daughters that we believe each individual is directly responsible to the Lord. Yes, he may be the victim of many unfortunate circumstances, and may have personality problems due to factors of heredity and environment, but the fact remains that each individual is morally and spiritually accountable to God, and will stand before Him for judgment. But let us also fulfill in ourselves the biblical demand that our lives be marked by the self-sacrificial love of Jesus, who not only showed us His own love, but also said, "A new commandment I give unto you, that ye love one another" (John 13:34).

If our sons and daughters see spiritual reality in our daily conduct, and know that we love them to the point that we would die for them if necessary, they will love us in return, share their deepest problems with us, submit to our discipline, and accept our teaching.

7

PARENTAL GUIDANCE—
The Boy-Girl Relationship

PARENTS of teen-agers often face serious problems just because the sinful human race is composed of male and female. Much has been written about the school or church providing sex education, but Christian parents should realize that the responsibility to teach their children rests primarily upon their shoulders. The attitudes formed during the earliest years of a child's life are tremendously important. Most teens who have received good spiritual instruction and genuine biblical training will live by sound moral principles, and will regard sex as a sacred gift from God. But many Christian parents have not provided a proper atmosphere for their children, often arguing and many times manifesting little tender love toward one another. Such mothers and fathers may be in for trouble when their children reach the teens.

Another factor to be considered is the undeniable fact that not every boy and girl who grows up in a Christian home is physically attractive. Nor does each young person possess a winsome personality. Many young believers have a poor self-image for one reason or another, and are not fully accepted by their peers. As a result, they reach out for friends

among others who likewise feel lonely and unwanted. These companions are often chosen without consideration for their spiritual background or
religious beliefs. Therefore, some of the teens in
our churches, though they once made what appeared
to be a sincere profession of faith in Christ, are now
dating young people who come from homes where
no semblance of religious training was ever given
and where no love is ever seen. Christian parents,
aware that their sons and daughters are unable or
unwilling to find their best friends among the young
people who go to church, wonder what they should
do.

Another circumstance causing Christian parents
concern is the innate desire of young people to be
accepted and popular. Attractive and talented teen-
agers want to be looked upon as "cool." To gain rec-
ognition they are often tempted to date nonchristians
or engage in petting. They expect to retain their
purity and hope to establish a Christian home when
they get married, but right now they are willing to
make some minor concessions in their standards to
achieve popularity.

In our discussions of boy-girl relationships we will
deal with certain matters that may not even come
up in many homes. As stated earlier, young people who have been well trained and given a good
example will often pass through the time of dating
and courtship without causing distress or heartbreak
to their folks. But, as indicated, in many homes the
child's early training was deficient, and sometimes
the teen has psychological problems stemming from
physical appearance or personality defects. Difficult
situations are likely to arise, and parents must know
what to do. It is largely for their benefit that this
chapter has been written.

SET A GOOD EXAMPLE

Even a couple that has made many mistakes when their children were small—while they may not fully undo the harm already inflicted—can begin to set a good example before their teen-age children. With God's help, they can show that they love each other and that married people living in obedience to the laws of God can be happy.

Remember, marital love is not a magical experience. It is a commitment. If you realize this, you will avoid the mistakes of many husbands and wives. Pastors can testify that often men have come to them saying something like this: "I know my wife is a good person, a wonderful mother, and faithful to me. But somehow, I am not able to love her the way I should. I just don't think we are compatible."

Women, even from Christian homes, will say, "My husband is a good provider and generally kind to me and the children. Yet I believe that something is missing in our marriage, and am quite sure that if we could be divorced, I would be able to find someone else who could make me much happier."

Such statements reveal an immature and woefully inadequate concept of marriage. Marital love is a commitment made rationally as the result of a choice by both the husband and the wife. Therefore, every Christian man can love his wife, and every believing woman can love her husband. The Lord does not command us to do that which is impossible, and He said, "Husbands, love your wives, even as Christ also loved the church, and gave Himself for it" (Eph. 5:25). "Teach the young women to be sober-minded, to love their husbands, to love their children" (Titus 2:4).

A man and woman who share a mutual faith in Christ need not live together as virtual strangers merely tolerating one another for the sake of the children. If they wish to do so, they can establish a real and deep love relationship. In some cases it may be necessary to seek counsel from a mature and experienced person, whether a pastor or Christian psychologist, but it is never necessary for two believers either to continue living together in a loveless home, or to obtain a divorce. To take one of these courses is to deny God's transforming power in the life of a believer. If you are the parents of teens, therefore, and you haven't been living the way a husband and wife should, pray with one another, talk to one another, and seek professional help if necessary, and by all means be sure you rekindle the flame of love.

Your teen needs to see that you are in love with one another and that you enjoy being together. He should be able to detect love in your eyes as you look at one another, hear it in the tone of your voice as you speak, and observe it in the way you act. Never argue in his presence, and never be competitive for his affection. Agree and support one another in matters of discipline, and show your teen-ager that marriage can be a wonderful relationship with a unity of love, purpose, and interest. He needs to know that you really love one another, and that you are very happy.

DISCUSS CURRENT PROBLEMS

In addition to showing their teens that they are in love, Christian parents must be able to discuss sex-oriented problems with them. Our young people are growing up in a society which strongly emphasizes sex, and they are far more sophisticated on the subject than we were at their age. Advertisements in magazines and on television use sex appeal to sell toothpaste, cars, insurance, and other products really not sexually oriented. Scantily dressed women and brazenly suggestive songs and slogans are the order of the day. Pornographic literature is readily available to our teens, and undoubtedly many of them have already seen pictures which explicitly depict the sex act.

You must also remember that young people today freely discuss subjects like birth control, abortion, and homosexuality. Teens from Christian homes often hear their companions at school brag about their sexual exploits. In some cases girls from homes where no moral principles are taught are taking birth control pills so they won't become pregnant. They tell others that they are having fun without risk. Four-letter words and crude terms for coitus are used freely, and the philosophy that intercourse is nothing more than a biological function involving two bodies is expressed widely. The current philosophy of our sex-oriented society is making a profound impression upon our young people. Great pressure is being put upon them to conform. After all, they desire popularity and prestige. Besides, they are naturally curious, and possess physical urges which must be kept under control.

Dr. Robert E. Fitch states the situation well:

When we turn away from the frauds and the illusions to the realities of the present scene, one fact stands out: young people today are losing control of their lives. They are having babies when they don't want them. They are getting married before they really want to. They are taking jobs before they are adequately prepared for them. And this is the "new freedom"! But freedom is precisely what is being lost. There is pathos in the life of anyone who has cheated himself of the freedom really to choose to get married, to choose to have a baby, to choose to take a job. ("The Sexplosion," *Christian Century,* January 29, 1964.)

In view of the situation, Christian parents cannot maintain a discreet silence on the subject of sex. They must discuss the issues with their sons and daughters, clearly setting forth the Christian view.

EMPHASIZE MORAL STANDARDS

Christian parents should make no apology for emphasizing the old-fashioned moral standards taught in the Bible. Charlie Shedd, in his popular book, *The Stork Is Dead,* gives a great deal of sound advice, but I do not agree with his premise that we should "talk first about what's smart, not right and wrong." Many young people will be able to rationalize themselves into a sexual relationship on this basis. Unless they are thoroughly convinced that premarital sex is sinful, they will often be inclined to think their situation is somewhat special and different from that of others.

Then, too, they are being told that one can enjoy sex without love before marriage just for the pleasure involved, and that this will in no way prevent falling in love, marrying, and enjoying a more satisfying relationship later. To counteract these falsehoods, parents must clearly communicate the moral truths of God, and point out from the Bible that such things as fornication and adultery are sinful and displeasing to God.

The Scriptures are explicit in their teaching, making it clear that sexual sins are especially revolting in God's sight. Paul declared, "Flee fornication. Every sin that a man doeth is outside the body; but he that committeth fornication sinneth against his own body" (1 Cor. 6:18). Sexual impurity is especially degrading when committed by a Christian because the Holy Spirit indwells the believer's body. It is God's temple, and to make it the very instrument of sin is a grievous insult to the Almighty. The primary reason young people should avoid having premarital sexual relations is that it is sin in the sight of God.

THE PERILS OF PERMISSIVENESS

Once the truth has been established that intercourse by unmarried people is forbidden by God, it is well to point out that permissiveness is inflicting a heavy toll on society. Mental and emotional disorders among college students are making necessary the services of more and more psychologists and psychiatrists. Hospitals for people who have mental disorders are overcrowded, and Dr. Francis Braceland, former president of the American Psychiatric Association and currently editor of the *American Journal of Psychiatry,* laid part of the blame for the situation on the permissiveness of our society. He said, "A more lenient attitude about premarital sex experience has posed stresses upon some women severe enough to cause emotional breakdowns."

More than 200,000 cases of venereal disease are treated every year, and illegal abortions have become the scandal of our times. Thousands of children are the victims of broken homes, caused by sexual infidelity on the part of a parent. Homosexuals are becoming more and more bold, and the acceptance of their deviant behavior will have the same disastrous effect upon our civilization that it did upon the Graeco-Roman world of Christ's day. It is easy to see that the moral fiber of our nation is being weakened, and a study of history shows that this condition usually precedes the fall of a civilization.

THE SELFISHNESS OF PERMISSIVENESS

The "playboy philosophy," popularized by Hugh Hefner, is clearly condemned by the Scriptures. It is basically selfish and totally unfulfilling. The

young male is encouraged to make as many conquests as he can, both to fulfill his sexual drive and
to bolster his ego. The girl is expected to give her
body to someone who does not necessarily love her,
and who may never want her as his own. Sexual freedom for young and attractive people is glamorized,
but nothing is provided for those who are not physically appealing or have passed the middle years of
life.

The failure of the "playboy philosophy" to provide real happiness has become apparent. Thousands of men and women have found that they could
not experience true happiness through illicit love-
making. The merely physical aspect of sex did not
provide what they were looking for. They needed the
feeling of being loved and wanted far more than
they needed the physical gratification of their pas-
sions.

THE BIBLICAL PURPOSE OF SEX

In addition to showing teen-agers that marital love
is beautiful and provides real happiness, Christian
parents must also set forth the positive emphasis of
the Scriptures on the subject of sex. It is a gift from
God intended to enrich human life and to provide
the means for the continuation of the race. The
Bible declares that God made us "male and female,"
and that the sexual relationship and marriage were
ordained before the Fall. "And Adam said, This is
now bone of my bones, and flesh of my flesh; she
shall be called Woman, because she was taken out
of Man. Therefore shall a man leave his father and
his mother, and shall cleave unto his wife; and they
shall be one flesh. And they were both naked, the
man and his wife, and were not ashamed" (Gen.
2:23-25).

The beauty of marriage is confirmed throughout
the Scriptures, and the writer of Hebrews said,

"Marriage is honorable in all, and the bed undefiled" (Heb. 13:4).

The marriage relationship is compared in the book of Ephesians to that bond which exists between Christ and the church. Within marriage, two human beings can find the deepest and most significant expression of human love. Christian parents should make sure their children understand these simple but basic biblical truths about sex and marriage.

DATING

In our sex-oriented society, boys and girls begin to take an interest in one another long before they are teens. Many 12- and 13-year-olds have already gained a great deal of knowledge about sex. Some have also achieved physical maturity to the point where it is possible for them to engage in intercourse. Their knowledge and physical development, combined with their emotional instability, present a dangerous combination.

DON'T PUSH

Group activities involving boys and girls help develop a proper attitude toward the opposite sex. These should be encouraged if properly supervised. Parents, however, must be careful that they do not instigate a pairing off of teen-agers. The Lord has placed natural instincts within them which will bring about the desire for a one-to-one relationship soon enough. Mothers of attractive young girls should not encourage them to be flirtatious. Nor should parents think it is cute when a pretty daughter begins to imitate the girls who provide the sex appeal in advertisements. Sometimes mothers are so afraid their daughters will be unclaimed that they push them into becoming somewhat seductive at a very early age. The girl doesn't fully realize what she is doing to boys, and trouble can develop.

ASK QUESTIONS

Christian parents should not be afraid to ask questions of their teens when they are planning to go on a date or attend a group activity. With whom will you be? Where are you going? What time will the activity end? What do you plan to do afterward? These are valid questions, and the teen-ager should expect them. The answers will help you determine whether or not you will allow him or her to go. The information will also enable you to establish a fair curfew.

Young people sometimes object to answering parental queries. They may say you are treating them as if they were little children. They might even show anger on some occasions. Do not let this dissuade you, however, for down in their hearts they know you are doing what is right, and they are glad that you care that much about them.

A girl of 16 had parents who were known to be unreasonable in their restrictions. In her Sunday School class, a number of the young people complained about the rules in their own homes, and one of the fellows said that he wished his folks would forget all about the curfew. The 16-year-old replied, "I really don't think you would like that. I sometimes am unhappy with the demands my parents make, but actually I am glad to know that they love me enough to care. I talk to kids at school whose folks never ask where they are going and never tell them when to come home. One boy said it makes him wonder if his parents are really interested in him. He felt that if he were in an accident, he could lie alongside the road all night without his folks even realizing he hadn't come home. He said they wouldn't miss him until they got up for work in the morning. It made him feel badly to think that this was all he meant to them. I am sure he would rather have his parents be overly strict than the way they are."

As long as your children are under your parental roof and are your dependents, you have the right to demand that they obey you. You can set a reasonable time for them to come in, and it is perfectly proper for you to forbid them to go out with certain people or carry out some of their plans. It may not always be easy to make the right decision, but a combination of firmness and love, strengthened by a dependence upon Christ, will enable you to handle properly your teen's dating activity.

Far more people fail their teens by being too permissive than by being too strict. It is better to say no on some occasions when you might have said yes than to say yes when your answer should have been no. Earlier in this book we stated that you do not alienate permanently a son or daughter when you teach him or her how to live responsibly. If your teen is convinced that you are honestly seeking his welfare, he will not hate you. He may sometimes think you are making a mistake, but he will really be glad that you love him enough to forbid something when it would have been much easier for you to grant permission.

GOING STEADY

The trend today is for young people to go steady at an early age. It gives status, a certain amount of self-confidence, freedom from apprehension regarding a companion at formal affairs, someone to lean upon and share life's experiences with, and a degree of emotional enrichment at a very early age. Some parents are quite relieved when they see their teenager dating one person steadily, especially if they think the individual will make a good mate. A teen with a steady date often appears quite happy, and may present his parents with relatively few difficult problems.

A number of hazards are involved in going steady too early, however, and we ought to be aware of them. Dr. William S. Deal, a professional counselor in marriage, family, and youth relations, lists in his book *Counseling Christian Parents* five reasons why going steady too young is not good:

(1) *"It may warp the personalities of the young people involved."*

When teens become involved with only one person, they do not develop good friendships with others. They like to be with their special friend, and as a result miss out on the benefits of sharing the experiences of many normally adjusted, healthy personalities. If these two young people get married, they most likely will continue to be loners. They will withdraw themselves from social activities at church or in connection with their work. Both may suffer periods of depression.

The romance may end before marriage if one of the parties matures in his thinking. But when this happens, both will find it very difficult to get back into the groups where new friendships can be established and a new mate discovered.

(2) *"Often the girl is exposed to the possibility of a premarital pregnancy."*

Young people who are not happy or who think their parents are treating them unfairly tend to find all their comfort in that one individual with whom they have been going steady. The likelihood of their becoming physically intimate and "going all the way" is great indeed. Often their illicit intercourse will continue until the girl becomes pregnant.

(3) *"Sometimes a young person gets 'stuck' with an emotionally disturbed person who begs pitifully not to be ditched."*

Dr. Deal says that such a person is definitely in need of professional help, and that the sooner he gets it, the better his chances for recovery.

(4) *"Going steady too young may not only warp the personality, engender too early marriages, throw the girl in danger of premarital pregnancy, but may also hinder one in finding the proper mate."*

It is perhaps too much to expect a 15-year-old to make a mature decision regarding marriage. True, some childhood romances blossom into a lifetime of marital happiness, but more often this is not the case. Two young people not well-suited to one another decide to marry, but both parties feel that somehow they have made a mistake. Even if they remain together, their home will not be all it ought to be.

(5) *"Going steady too young can also become an educational hazard."*

Teen-agers who are thinking of an early marriage are often willing to forgo their education to get a job that offers very little by way of real benefits or satisfaction. They tend to sacrifice their future on the altar of the present.

It is difficult to lay down absolutes when dealing with the subject of early courtships and marriages. As noted before, they do not always turn out badly. All parents, however, should be aware of the hazards involved, keep in touch with their teens, and give whatever guidance they can when their boys or girls are going steady.

DATING NONCHRISTIANS

When teens begin to seek the company of the opposite sex, this question often arises: "What about dating kids who are not Christians?" Young people genuinely committed to Christ come into daily contact with many who have never really given the matter much thought. In fact, close friendships sometimes are formed between believers and nonbelievers, and we do not discourage such associations as long as our teens do not compromise their position. In fact, we tell our youth to be good witnesses for Christ by word and example. Dating is different, however, because it may lead to romance and marriage. Therefore, we must warn our teenagers about the dangers of going out on dates with someone who isn't a Christian.

A fine young person who truly loves Christ may think that a few casual dates with an unsaved teen will have no serious repercussions. A fondness often develops very quickly, however, and before long the two young people fall in love. When this happens, the pleas of parents and the admonitions of a pastor fall on deaf ears. The two are now in love, and they feel it would be impossible for them to reverse the situation.

Occasionally the nonbeliever becomes a Christian before the wedding takes place. This doesn't usually happen, however, and a Christian young person should never begin dating someone who doesn't know Christ with the fond hope that that individual will soon be saved. More often than not, the nonbeliever will simply declare that he or she is not quite ready to make a decision about salvation. Worse still, the nonbeliever may make an insincere profession of faith just to please some of the relatives and make it possible for the wedding to take place in the church. We know that many pastors are placed in a difficult position when they have sincere doubts about the genuineness of a so-called "decision for Christ," but must proceed with wedding plans because they cannot judge the heart.

THE BIBLE AND MIXED MARRIAGE

The Scriptures clearly teach that a believer is not to marry an unbeliever. In the Old Testament, for example, God strictly forbade the marriage of the Hebrews and the heathen. (See Deuteronomy 7:3; Joshua 23: 12-13; Ezra 9:12; Nehemiah 13:25.)

In the New Testament, Paul specifically declared that if a widow desires to marry, she may do so as long as it is "in the Lord" (1 Cor. 7:39). He also set forth a principle applicable to marriage when he said, "Be ye not unequally yoked together with unbelievers; for what fellowship hath righteousness with unrighteousness? And what communion hath light with darkness?" (2 Cor. 6:14).

Christian parents have an obligation to instruct their teen-agers to be very careful not to fall in love with an unbeliever. Young people should realize that a marriage between a Christian and one who is not is a violation of God's law, and is not likely to produce real happiness.

FACING A BAD SITUATION

The combined efforts of parents, pastors, and other friends sometimes cannot prevent a marriage between a believer and a nonbeliever. When this happens, some mothers and fathers become so enraged that they reject both their own son or daughter and the mate. They belligerently declare they will have nothing to do with them. Others, though expressing their disapproval, finally bow to the inevitable. They treat the pair with courtesy and kindness, participate in the wedding, and maintain close contact after marriage.

The second course of action is certainly the wiser

of the two. In some cases, parents can be of inestimable help in leading the new "in-law" to Christ.

Instances can be cited to illustrate the truth that when parents pray and show love, God's transforming grace can bring about the establishment of a good home for their children. A woman who was not a Christian married a regenerated but backslidden young man. A short time ago she declared that she came to know the Lord a few years after the marriage through the testimony and kindness of her mother-in-law. She saw so much love, purity, and genuine sweetness in her husband's mother that she became attracted to the Saviour. The husband came back into fellowship with the Lord, and the two were able to rear a fine family in a truly Christian home.

INTERRACIAL DATING

Interracial dating is bound to become more common in our increasingly integrated world. Recent surveys indicate that 75 percent of our population still disapprove of marriages between whites and nonwhites. It appears that the feeling is similar regardless of race. A large number of blacks insist that "black is beautiful," and they are just as opposed to racial intermarriage as many white people. It is well for us to be informed on this issue, so that we can talk about it with our teen-agers.

First, let us make sure that our position is free from prejudice. Christian parents should also avoid making statements that have no basis in fact. Some years ago it was common to hear that black people were far more animallike in their sex drives, but no evidence can be found to support such claims. Therefore, not a single word should ever be uttered by a white believer which makes him sound as if he thinks that yellow-skinned, brown-skinned, or black-skinned people are inferior.

Interracial dating, however, carries with it strong potential for an unhappy marriage. The problem would be one of adjustment, because of certain factors built into our society.

It is well for us to bear in mind that even when two people of the same class, race, and denomination establish a home, they may face real problems of adjustment. Whenever any element of dissimilarity is added, the process of harmonization becomes more difficult. Some blacks resent intermarriage as a betrayal of their race, and some whites interpret it as a breaking down of a separation God has established. Then, too, the backgrounds of two people from different races may be so diverse that both will be forced to make major changes. Interracial dating, therefore, may bring on a number of serious problems.

OTHER DENOMINATIONS

Christian parents should also talk to their teens about the matter of dating young people of other denominations. For example, if a young man who attends a liturgical church meets a girl who has been raised in a less formal fellowship, they may be in for some problems if they become serious with one another. They may be deeply in love and share a common devotion to Christ, but one or both of them will find it necessary to make many adjustments in relation to their faith. It will be difficult to find a church home which will suit them both. Therefore, it is always best to keep in mind that dating leads to romance and that romance leads to marriage. Make sure your teen-agers understand this.

THE PREGNANT TEEN

The pregnant teen-aged girl is one of the most upsetting and difficult situations Christian parents ever encounter. The mingled feelings of grief, shame, disappointment, frustration, and perplexity may cause a mother or father to react in an extremely emotional manner, and make harsh and cruel statements which may be regretted later.

"Now you've brought shame and disgrace upon us and the rest of the family. I hope you are satisfied."

"You've been a problem to us from the time you were little. Now you top it off with this."

"As far as I'm concerned, you're not my daughter anymore. I don't care what you do, just get out of my life."

Of course, no truly Christian parent really wishes to disown an unmarried daughter because she is pregnant. But people often say things they don't really mean when ashamed or angry. At such a time the girl needs the reassurance of her parents' love and genuine concern more than ever.

Teen-age pregnancy often occurs when a girl feels insecure or is rebellious. As mentioned earlier, teens who have a feeling of loneliness and a poor self-image like to go steady at a very early age, and find much comfort and satisfaction through this special one-to-one relationship with a young person of the opposite sex. They share their problems with one another, and really don't feel secure and happy unless they are together. This is why such a situation often leads to pregnancy.

Girls with a poor self-image sometimes become the victims of popular boys who use them for sexual gratification with no intention of ever marrying them. In fact, it is common for fellows to brag about their conquests, and soon everyone knows the "easy numbers." A girl eager to be accepted by a boy whom all the girls consider to be "cool" often thinks she will help her chances by giving in to his demands for sex.

Then, too, sometimes girls who are rebellious and feel a keen dislike for their parents will seek revenge by going all the way with a boy. It is a way of hurting mother and dad. She may feel guilty afterward, but the next time she is angry and thinks her folks have been unfair, she is likely to repeat her performance.

SHOW LOVE AND CONCERN

When a teen-age girl becomes pregnant, she is often frightened and bewildered. She does not understand her feelings as she realizes that a new life she didn't want is developing within her body. If she comes from a Christian home, she will have deep feelings of guilt and a certain amount of shame. Her parents, the pastor, and others to whom she looks for help should show her that they still love her, and point out that though she has sinned, she can be forgiven and still become a fine Christian woman. She desperately needs acceptance, and encouragement for the future.

It will also be necessary for her to receive advice and counsel. She is faced with four options: (1) to marry the boy responsible, (2) to have the baby and live with it at home in hopes that she will meet a young man who will love her enough to marry her and adopt the child, (3) to have an abortion, (4) to have the baby placed in a Christian home through an adoption agency.

AN IMMEDIATE MARRIAGE

Often the best solution is marriage to the boy involved. If he has been dating her steadily, has the same religious beliefs, loves her, and really wants to marry her, no other option should be considered. A young man can do a great deal of growing up in a short time even if he has to drop out of school for a year or two so that he may shoulder his new responsibilities as a husband and father.

Some people may be shocked at the idea of someone interrupting his schooling, but this is not necessarily a tragedy. It will actually be good for this young fellow to earn a living for himself and his family through hard work. If he is a good student and is properly motivated, he can always go back to school to complete his education.

Parents must allow the young couple to face responsibilities themselves. After the initial shock has worn off, mothers and dads may be inclined to become overly generous and helpful, but this would be a mistake. You can show kindness to them by giving some small gifts and offering a limited amount of help. But do not allow them to sidestep their own responsibilities. If you shower them with material favors, you will slow up the maturing process.

The teen-aged couple might need counseling from an experienced pastor or Christian psychologist. We have said earlier that teens who go steady at an early age often do so because they are lonely, insecure, and have a poor self-image. The young couple needs to be encouraged to attend the Sunday services in church, and to participate in fellowship gatherings with other young marrieds. They must realize that friends are important, and that they will never achieve the highest level of happiness if they isolate themselves from others.

RAISING THE BABY AT HOME

When a teen-aged girl becomes pregnant, marriage is not always possible or wise. The boy who is responsible may not be emotionally ready for marriage, may not love the girl, or may have a totally different outlook upon life. Sometimes when a girl is pregnant because she was rebellious, the man is older or already married. In such a situation, she may choose to have the baby and raise it at home. She will be hoping and praying that sometime in the near future a young man will fall in love with her, marry her, and adopt the child.

This occasionally works out well, but it is really not fair to the girl's parents, her baby, or her prospective husband. Her mother and father should not be saddled with this kind of responsibility, and the infant will spend his earliest years in an abnormal situation. Such a child may develop strong feelings for the grandparents, so that when the time comes to leave them, the experience will be deeply traumatic. Besides, when a young fellow and his wife begin their home, the presence of a baby sired by another man could be a disrupting factor. The husband may never be able to have the same feeling for this child as for those that are born later.

THE POSSIBILITY OF ABORTION

When an unmarried teen becomes pregnant, many counselors advise an early abortion. They say that even if the girl and boy love one another, they should not have a child arriving a few months after their marriage. Furthermore, they insist that no woman should be forced to bear a baby she doesn't really want, and that with overpopulation a problem, it just makes good sense to terminate all undesirable pregnancies by an abortion.

These arguments may sound convincing to a pregnant young girl who is afraid as she thinks of the future. Yet the fact remains that abortion involves the taking of "life." One cannot properly equate the expulsion of the fetus with the removal of a gallbladder or appendix. This fact should be clearly explained to every girl considering an abortion.

THE SACREDNESS OF LIFE

Christians have always looked upon human life as

sacred. In this we stand in sharp contrast to the
attitudes of many today. This was also true in the
Early Church, for the pagans of Greece and Rome
had absolutely no scruples against either abortion or
infanticide. From its very beginning, however, the
Christian faith has taken a negative stand on abortion.

Dr. David R. Mace writes in his book

One of our best sources of information about
what was going on lies in the early Christian writings and the fact that they so often condemned
their pagan neighbors for both abortion and infanticide. This would not have been necessary if
these practices had not been fairly common. The
Christian Church from the beginning regarded
abortion as a serious sin.

The Teachings of the Twelve Apostles, one of
the earliest Christian writings outside the New
Testament, said plainly, "You shall not slay a
child by abortion. You shall not kill what is
generated." Similar passages appear in other early
Christian writings. *The Apocalypse of Peter* speaks
of women "who have caused their children to be
born untimely and have corrupted the work of
God who created them." This theme occurs again
and again—life is given directly by God, and
must not be destroyed. This attitude contrasted
sharply with the widespread pagan view that the
lives of people of low degree—especially of slaves
and of infants—were not of any special value.

What about the Hebrew attitude? The only
reference to abortion in the Old Testament is in
Exodus 21:22, which refers to the man who accidentally hurts a woman so that he terminates
her pregnancy. The implication is that *deliberate*
termination of pregnancy would be unthinkable.
The divine commandment to be "fruitful and mul-
tiply" gave the Hebrews a profound respect for

child life, which they considered as a special gift from God. The high Christian value placed upon early life undoubtedly had its roots in this Hebrew attitude.

The absence of direct references to abortion in the New Testament strongly suggests that it was not practiced to any significant degree in the Jewish community. It was only later, when Christians lived in closer contact with the pagan community of the Roman Empire, that vigorous attacks on abortion began to be made. *(Abortion: The Agonizing Decision.)*

It is apparent, therefore, that Christians have never viewed abortion as proper. The endless discussion about the exact time the fetus receives its eternal spirit has not provided specific guidelines. The Christian view of human life as a sacred gift from God is decidedly against abortion.

In this chapter we need not discuss the subject of therapeutic abortion, nor exceptional situations, like a girl being raped by a psychopath. More than 99 percent of pregnant teen-age girls are neither the victims of rape nor candidates for a therapeutic abortion. In almost every instance, the girl can give birth to a normal baby.

The argument that the overpopulation crisis demands all premarital pregnancies to be terminated by abortion has little validity. True, Christians are concerned about the problem of overpopulation, and many are limiting the size of their families. But this does not mean that we have the right to resort to abortion as a means of controlling population growth. Besides, a sensitive girl who is convinced that life is sacred, should she undergo an abortion, could very well go through the rest of her life with a troubled conscience and deep feelings of guilt. Abortion is not the answer to a teen-age pregnancy.

PLACING FOR ADOPTION

When a teen-ager is pregnant, and marriage is not deemed advisable, one of the best solutions is for the prospective mother to visit a Christian adoption agency and make arrangements for the child to be placed in a good home. Many fine couples who love the Lord and are unable to have children of their own are seeking a baby through adoption. They will give the infant all the love and care it needs to grow up as a well-adjusted and happy child.

Seeing our sons and daughters through the boy-girl problems of the teen years can be a wonderful experience. It can also be a period of heartbreak and disappointment. Much will depend upon the example we set and the training we gave our children in their earliest years. But other factors such as their talents, weaknesses, looks, and psychological make-up may also be contributing elements.

In any case, let us pray for them, study the Bible, be faithful in church, and live as real Christians before them. Let us show them that true happiness comes through doing the will of God. Let us be honest, open, and firm when necessary, but also kind and forgiving. And, even if some very difficult experiences come our way, let us rest upon the assurances and promises of God's Word.

8

CHRISTIAN RESPONSIBILITY—
Helping the Delinquent Teen

IN THIS final chapter we will discuss the problem of teen-agers who become lawbreakers. Because of the rapid rise in the rate of juvenile delinquency, this topic should be of vital interest to all Christians, though most parents who have lived godly lives and trained their children well do not face this difficulty in their own homes. I am thinking of the young person who rebels against authority, rejects the "establishment," sneers at organized religion, and has clashed with school officials or law enforcement agencies. A large number of teens, some from good homes, can be classified as delinquents, and we should be genuinely concerned about them.

In considering our subject, we will first try to understand why young people go wrong, so that we can better help the overall situation. We will then think specifically about delinquent teens from Christian homes, and set forth biblical guidelines for parents and all other concerned individuals.

SOCIETY AND CHRISTIAN RESPONSIBILITY

We must recognize that environment plays a major role in causing delinquency. A large percentage of the young who break the law and feel bitterness toward the adult world come from the slums of our large cities. As Christians, we must not immunize ourselves from the problems of those who live in dire poverty and distressing conditions.

Thousands grow up in ghetto districts as part of a family that lives on meager earnings or welfare grants. Since Christians have done little to evangelize such areas, these people have seldom had contact with the Gospel. Parents in such a location often have low moral values and many are totally ignorant of spiritual truths. They are unable, therefore, to give their children the kind of training that is needed. Their boys and girls, upon reaching the middle and later teens, find it difficult to obtain a job. As a result, they are likely to wander about aimlessly, develop an attitude of indifference to work, fall in with older companions, and become involved in drugs, immorality, and crime. Boys find stealing cars both lucrative and exciting, and girls often become adept at shoplifting or are easily led into giving sex for whatever advantages they can gain.

We must not underestimate the seriousness of these environmental factors. A Christian youth worker recently said that he was personally acquainted with a number of fellows from the ghettos who did well when they were in the armed forces. But he said that when they returned home and were unable to find employment, many became very discouraged and gradually drifted into irresponsible behavior and lawbreaking activities.

The apparent hopelessness of the total situation certainly contributes to this kind of life, and believers should become involved. Christ-centered evangelistic efforts and worthy programs of compassion for depressed areas should be supported by people who know and love the Lord Jesus. Teen-age delinquency would be greatly reduced if Christians would carry out the great commission in the ghetto districts of our large cities.

PARENTAL RESPONSIBILITY

Another cause of delinquency among teens is a lack of proper training in the early years of childhood. Many parents in affluent circles are so engrossed with business and social activities that they pay little attention to their children. Beginning at infancy, they give the child everything he wants as a substitute for their own time and companionship. They seldom if ever assign tasks to their children and see that they are carried out. They show a lack of real concern for their child's welfare in school. As a result, the youngster enters his teens spoiled and overindulged. He is also insecure and unhappy, for he has never experienced the satisfaction of being needed, wanted, and genuinely helpful. He harbors resentment toward his parents, sees them as hypocrites, and is apt to try immorality, drugs, and even crime just for kicks.

By the time parents of such young people finally become aware of the situation, it has become very difficult to do anything about it. But hope still exists if they will acknowledge their failings and begin to show an interest in their teens. If Christian parents will teach and demonstrate what responsible living is according to the Scriptures, rebellious teens *can* be helped.

INDIVIDUAL RESPONSIBILITY

Though we acknowledge that social, economic, and domestic conditions are definitely factors in producing delinquents, we must always place a great deal of emphasis upon individual responsibility. Not all the young people who steal, use drugs, or are implicated in violent crimes come from the slums, nor in every case have they been overindulged by busy parents. It is obvious that personal choices are also involved.

For example, Gordon McLean in his book *God Help Me—I'm a Parent,* tells of two brothers only one year apart in age who were almost a direct contrast in the way they lived. Both attended the same school, and enjoyed the same privileges, but there the similarity ended. Rubin was active in athletics, did well in school, and respected his parents and others in authority over him. George, on the other hand, caused his mother and father much grief, did not do well scholastically, and was continually in trouble with the law. At the time Mr. McLean was writing his book, George was awaiting trial as a member of a group charged with burglary, robbery, conspiracy, and murder.

The story of these two boys graphically illustrates the fact of individual responsibility. Some people with wonderful opportunities, great talents, good looks, and many other plus factors do not take advantage of their good fortune. They choose the wrong pathway. Others with far less natural gifts and good circumstances grow up to become responsible citizens. Christian parents and others who are involved with delinquent teens should therefore make them recognize that they themselves are to blame for their problems, and that it will do them no good to place all the responsibility upon others. The wayward teen must be made to see that he failed to choose the right way, and that he could have done differently. Gordon McLean, experienced counselor of young people who have gotten themselves into trouble, says,

One young man, who evidently had been around treatment programs long enough to learn the jargon very well, summed it . . . one day: "I didn't steal a car because I had sibling rivalry, maternal conflicts, or psychotic tendencies. I stole the car because I wanted to go someplace, and stealing seemed to be the fastest way to get there. I knew it was wrong, I got caught, and now I'll just have to pay for what I did wrong. It's that simple." It may not be just that simple, but he's basically right. (from *God Help Me—I'm a Parent*, Creation House, 1972.)

TRUE KINDNESS

The parent whose teen is showing signs of becoming a delinquent is not really being kind when he allows him to blame society or says he simply needs psychological help. It may make the young person feel better for the moment if he can think he is not culpable for his condition, but it will not provide him any hope for the future.

Many people fail to see that the denial of individual accountability leads to hopelessness and despair. If the Freudian psychologists are right when they say you can't help being what you are, you must look upon yourself as just a victim of circumstances and as possessing no power to change anything. A folk song by Anna Russell in a humorous way sets forth the superficiality and emptiness of the modern Freudian approach to human behavior.

I went to my psychiatrist to be psychoanalyzed,
To find out why I killed the cat and blacked my
    husband's eyes.
He laid me on a downy couch to see what he
    could find,
And here is what he dredged up from my sub-
    conscious mind:

When I was one, my mommy hid my dolly
in a trunk,
And so it follows naturally that I am always
drunk.
When I was two, I saw my father kiss the maid
one day,
And that is why I suffer now from kleptomania.
At three, I had the feeling of ambivalence
toward my brothers,
And so it follows naturally, I poison all my
lovers.
But I'm happy, now I've learned the lesson this
has taught;
That everything I do that's wrong is someone
else's fault.

How much better it is to know that you yourself are
responsible for your bad conduct, and that you can
take steps to change the situation. Moreover, as
Christians we can set forth the glorious message of
full forgiveness and a new life. What an encouragement it is for someone in deep trouble because of
his sin to hear the words, "Come now, and let us
reason together, saith the Lord: though your sins
be as scarlet, they shall be as white as snow; though
they be red like crimson, they shall be as wool"
(Isa. 1:18). What hope for a new life of victory
springs up when one learns, "Therefore, if any man
be in Christ, he is a new creation; old things are
passed away; behold, all things are become new"
(2 Cor. 5:17).

THE NEED FOR FIRMNESS

While parents of a wayward and rebellious teen
must not make him feel that he has been rejected,
they must continue to be firm. They should be
friendly, tell him they love him, and let him know
that they deeply desire his happiness and welfare.

But they must never provide him with an excuse for his wrong attitudes and conduct.

It is also important that parents do not give the appearance of being weak by sending out pity signals. Sometimes mothers and fathers can feel sorry for themselves, and say something like, "Just think of what you are doing to me. After all I've done for you, how can you treat me this way?" These words, if uttered in a plaintive tone, will bring about an emotional and negative response. All your expressions of concern should be for him, and not for yourselves.

Be on guard also against becoming overly sympathetic when he sets forth a plausible argument blaming everyone else for the difficulty into which he has gotten himself. Do not allow him to sway your thinking and make you join him in denouncing his fellowmen. Any indication you give which permits him to blame others to the point of excluding any personal responsibility will hinder a real and significant change in his behavior.

LET HIM SUFFER

Sometimes parents must allow their delinquent teen to learn the hard way that sin pays bitter wages. This is not easy, for our natural instinct is to shield the people we love as much as possible. But the only effective remedy for some teen-agers is pain and a deep hurt.

Of course, this does not mean that a father and mother should desert a teen when he gets into some trouble. It is possible that if dad accompanies him when he must appear before a magistrate, pays his fine, and shows his son that he will stick with him, the lad will repent and turn his life over to God. In many instances, a crisis situation of this kind has proven to be a turning point in the life of a teen-ager.

A lasting change will be more likely, however, if the parents do not make the experience too easy. Before the fine is paid, the young person should be made to promise that he will work to refund the money to his parents, and that he will obey whatever conditions the court lays down. If he carries through his promises and changes his pattern of conduct, you can consider his encounter with the legal authorities to be a blessing in disguise.

Parents must also be alert to signs of hypocrisy in a teen. Sometimes a young person will take advantage of the kindness his mother and father show him. He will put on a front of remorse and make a start toward better behavior only because it serves his own purposes at the time. Before long, he secretly returns to some of his old ways, and soon he is in trouble again. When this next collision with the law takes place, the parents of the offending young man, while showing him that they continue to love him, should not be so ready to come up with the money as they were the first time. Though extenuating circumstances may be involved which would justify giving him still another opportunity, the time probably has come for the parents to let him suffer the full consequences of his wrongdoing. Juvenile homes, jails, and prisons are not usually effective in reforming people, but a time of confinement may be the means by which a young person reared in a Christian home is brought to his senses.

THE LAW OF NATURAL CONSEQUENCE

Almost everybody knows that natural law operates in the realm of everyday living. A person who drives himself beyond the limits of his strength is likely to experience a physical or emotional breakdown. A man who is consistently reckless or exceeds the speed limit with his car will quite likely become involved in an accident and will pay traffic fines. Children who do not study or who fail to pay attention in class will normally get poor grades on their report cards.

Dr. Bruce Narramore, in his book *Help! I'm a Parent* (Zondervan, 1972), points out that parents must sometimes utilize this natural principle in the disciplining of their children. He illustrates it by telling how he and his wife handled their little girl when, despite a number of warnings and spankings, she repeatedly nibbled on a bar of soap. One day they decided to let nature fulfill her role, and gritted their teeth as they watched their child chew on the bar until bubbles began to come out of her mouth and she started to cry in distress. Only then did they come to her rescue, but by this time her lips were beginning to swell and she had an upset stomach. She and her parents spent a miserable day, but she never ate soap again.

This principle is also applicable to teens. Sometimes parents must summon all their courage and let a young person learn the lesson of life the hard way. If parents have a son who is rebellious, and comes home with marijuana and beer and brazenly declares that he is going to do what he wants, they must clearly demonstrate that they are in charge. They should insist that he will not smoke marijuana or drink beer in their home. If he threatens to leave, they must not back down. They should assure him of their love, but must insist that they cannot and will not condone his behavior. In many instances such a teen will come to terms with the parental rules and remain at home. Chances are he will respect his mother and father even more for their stand.

Such a course of action naturally involves a risk when older teen-agers are involved. A young person may decide to leave and live in an apartment with others who are in the same rebellious mood as he. Christian parents may wonder if they have been too heartless, and may be concerned that they have pushed him down the road toward destruction. They might not sleep very well, but find themselves doing a great deal of praying day and night, for this kind of decision is never easy.

This is the proper stand to take, however, and oftentimes it produces the desired results. For example, Jesus told the story of a father who gave one of his sons a substantial amount of money upon request. The older man may have wondered if the lad would make good use of his new freedom. He may even have anticipated that the boy would get into deep trouble. But he turned the money over to him just the same. If the young man had not developed into a responsible adult during his time at home, it could be that the law of natural consequence was the only means that would be effective.

Here is the story:

"And he said, A certain man had two sons; and the younger of them said to his father, Father, give me the portion of goods that falleth to me. And he divided unto them his living. And not many days after that, the younger son gathered all together, and took his journey into a far country, and there wasted his substance with riotous living. And when he had spent all, there arose a mighty famine in that land; and he began to be in want. And he went and joined himself to a citizen of that country; and he sent him into his fields to feed swine. And he would fain have filled his belly with the husks that the swine did eat; and no man gave unto him. And when he came to himself, he said, How many of my father's hired servants have bread enough and to spare, and I perish with hunger! I will arise and go to my father, and will say unto him, Father, I have sinned against heaven, and before thee, and am no more worthy to be called thy son; make me as one of thy hired servants.

"And he arose, and came to his father. But when

he was yet a great way off, his father saw him, and had compassion, and ran, and fell on his neck, and kissed him. And the son said unto him, Father, I have sinned against heaven, and in thy sight, and am no more worthy to be called thy son. But the father said to his servants, Bring forth the best robe, and put it on him; and put a ring on his hand, and shoes on his feet. And bring the fatted calf, and kill it; and let us eat, and be merry. For this, my son, was dead, and is alive again; he was lost, and is found. And they began to be merry" (Luke 15:11-24).

The young man soon went through all his money, lost his fickle friends, and began to feed hogs just to keep body and soul together. But one day he reflected upon the situation, and realized that his own headstrong behavior had brought him to this deplorable state. Suddenly he grew up. He knew that he had acted like a foolish child and decided that the only sensible thing for him to do was to go home and ask forgiveness. God's law of natural consequences had done its work.

Most of us shy away from this method of discipline. It's easier to spank a little child than to see him become ill from eating too much soap. We would rather endure problems with our teens and even wait for them to come home at a late hour than wonder if they are hungry, cold, or on a drug-induced trip. It's hard to sleep when you think your son or daughter may be living in deep sin. Yet it may be necessary for you to allow the law of natural consequence to discipline someone you love very much.

If you have been faithful in your duties as a Christian parent, are praying earnestly, and are really seeking to do the Lord's will, you can safely entrust the one you love into His hands. He can teach that young person lessons in the school of experience which could be learned in no other way.

Claim God's promise, and place your confidence in Him. He has said, "Train up a child in the way he should go and, when he is old, he will not depart from it" (Prov. 22:6).

AN ENCOURAGING WORD

Christian parents of a delinquent son or daughter living away from home can find many reasons for an optimistic attitude. Remember, a person who has received good instruction in his childhood and is the object of continual prayer will find it difficult to continue in the ways of sin. The early religious training has made an indelible impression upon his personality, and the remembrances of the beautiful faith of his childhood days will return from time to time. The prayers of his parents and other concerned individuals are heard in heaven, and the Lord will bring pressures to bear upon the wayward one. Though he never forces the will, God does chasten and bring about a deep inner dissatisfaction with the ways of the world. Anyone who knows the truth and who once was sensitive to spiritual matters will never be able to find true enjoyment in the pleasures of sin. Even though he may come to the place where he declares that he doesn't believe in God, he will know that he is lying when he says it.

THE EXPERIENCE OF SOLOMON

Dr. G. Campbell Morgan sees in the book of Ecclesiastes a picture of a person who is living in defiance of his own convictions. He points out that the sobbing and agony of the book is the cry of a man refusing to obey the dictates of his heart. Solomon just could not be an atheist or agnostic, though he was trying to live as if he were one. In Ecclesiastes he expresses the distress of one who knows the truth but has not submitted himself to it.

But Solomon could not find the peace and satisfaction for which he was looking, and in his experiences we see something of what every young person who has turned his back upon the Christian faith will endure. Nothing he attempts will give satisfaction. He may try everything from a life of deep sin to one of high humanistic endeavor, but until he places his faith in Jesus Christ and lives in obedience to God's Word, he will never be truly happy.

No mother or father, brother or sister should give up hope for loved ones wandering far from God. Keep on praying, and show love whenever you have the opportunity. Through bitter experience, that young man or woman will learn that God alone can satisfy. When such a person returns, greet him the way the prodigal's father did his repentant son. Let him know that he is forgiven and fully accepted.

Someday many of the young people from Christian homes who are now serving Satan and living for the flesh will turn back to God. They will declare that the only way one obtains true happiness is by walking in obedience to the revealed will of God. They will have learned through experience the truth of the closing exhortation of Ecclesiastes. "Let us hear the conclusion of the whole matter: Fear God, and keep his commandments; for this is the whole duty of man. For God shall bring every work into judgment, with every secret thing, whether it be good, or whether it be evil" (Eccl. 12:13, 14).

CONCLUSION

As I FINISH this volume, let me remind every reader that the first step toward living a Christian life and experiencing the joy and peace of salvation is to acknowledge your sin and receive Jesus Christ as your Savior. He came to earth to destroy the tyranny of sin by His sinless life, to pay the price for your sins by His death on the cross, and to break the power of death by His resurrection. Therefore, if you have never entered into a personal relationship with Him, you should do so right now.

Bow your head in prayer and settle this matter of your soul's salvation. Here is a suggested word of prayer you might offer: "Lord Jesus, I know that I am a sinner and could never save myself. I believe You died for me and shed Your precious blood for my sin, and that You rose again from the dead. I am receiving You now as my Savior, my Lord, my only hope of salvation. Lord, be merciful to me a sinner, and save me according to the promise of Your Word. In Jesus' name. Amen."

If you pray this and really mean it, you are saved. The Bible says,

"For whosoever shall call upon the name of the Lord shall be saved" (Rom. 10:13).